CW01674279

The Essential First-Year Student Survival Guide on How to Thrive at College and University

With Tips, Budget Planner, Checklists, Food Hacks & More; Graduation Gift Book for High School Leavers

Cameron Craft

PEMBURY PEAK

Published by Pembury Peak: info@PemburyPeak.com

First Edition May 2024

This book is lovingly dedicated to our daughters, Gwen and Judy, who radiate brightness, beauty, and kindness. As they now face a world filled with new opportunities and experiences, we look forward to seeing where their life journey takes them. I also dedicate this book to my husband, Tom. Your unwavering support, love, and understanding mean everything to me. You are a life partner and a true companion in our journey together in every sense.

This book is a tribute to the joy and love you all bring into my life.

Contents

INTRODUCTION

So You're Off on Your Next Academic Adventure!

As you embark on this exciting journey into higher education, be it at a college or university, this guide is crafted to help you navigate the first year with confidence and ease. Whether your campus is small or large, urban or rural, the insights and strategies shared will empower you to make the most of your educational journey.

These years are about so much more than lectures and books; they offer a mosaic of experiences that will shape the person you become. They are about discovering new passions, building lifelong friendships, and learning to stand on your own feet. This is a time where late-night study sessions meet early morning classes, where you're pushed beyond your comfort zone, and where ambitions take flight.

This guide is about thriving, not just surviving. It aims to provide practical advice using the wisdom of those who have walked this path before you. Think of it as a roadmap to navigate the complexities of student life, from managing your finances to finding your crowd, from staying healthy in body and mind to balancing the demands of coursework and the allure of the wider campus experience. Welcome to your new adventure - let's make it extraordinary!

Before we start, let's highlight some core elements to keep in mind:

Carpe Diem - Make These Years Count! Dive into the wealth of opportunities and activities, enriching your personal growth and expanding your horizons.

Balance & Well-Being: Master the art of time management - juggling academics, activities, and self-care, reducing stress, and promoting a healthy, balanced lifestyle.

Mentors Matter: Cultivate meaningful relationships with peers, professors, and advisors to establish a valuable network of support and opportunity.

Network Like Crazy! Start building connections early. The friendships and relationships formed during these years can be pivotal for the future; plus, they help develop communication and social skills.

Studying Must Be Your Priority! While it is important to join clubs and embrace new experiences, remember that academic success provides the groundwork for your future.

Enjoy the Ride! During this time, you'll experience a unique blend of challenges, triumphs, friendships, and fun. Savor the moments as memories will last long after graduation. Make the most of this unique time to the fullest!

Note for Readers: "College" vs. "University" Terminology

In this guide, we use the term "college" to encompass all higher education institutions. We appreciate that terminology varies between people and places, and some readers may be more familiar with or prefer the term "university." By choosing the term "college," we aim to maintain consistency and clarity throughout this guide, ensuring that the insights provided are universally applicable, regardless of your preferred institutional term. We appreciate your understanding.

CHAPTER 1

THE COUNTDOWN BEGINS: PREPARE FOR DEPARTURE!

" Before anything else, preparation is the key to success."

Alexander Graham Bell

Going to college is an exciting step in life, full of new experiences and opportunities. As you prepare to leave home, it is crucial to remember that this change does not happen overnight. Planning and preparing for the shift from high school to college is essential for a smooth transition.

Preparing for college involves several steps, such as deciding what to bring to your dorm, including academic materials and personal items. You must also prepare financially with a budget and bank account and plan for potential employment options. Connecting with your future roommates and staying in touch with your family is also crucial. Planning how you will get to college, whether driving, flying, or taking other public transportation, is essential.

Even though each area requires attention, there is no need to feel overwhelmed! Do your best to organize as soon as possible to facilitate a smooth transition. The following sections highlight crucial aspects that should be considered. At the end, a preparation timetable is suggested. So, let's start by breaking it down into manageable steps to make your departure for college as smooth and stress-free as possible.

Know Your Accommodation Setup

Ensuring that you settle in faster and are comfortable in your accommodation is helped by understanding your living situation before setting foot on campus. Here are some key reasons:

Plan Your Space: Dorm rooms are typically small, so knowing what space you have to work with is important. Some colleges provide the dimensions and layout of rooms, which can help you decide how to organize your belongings. Do research online for images, virtual tours, or videos posted by students of their dorm rooms at your college. Also, reach out to your college's housing department or landlord (if living off-campus) for this information if it's not readily available.

What To Pack: Knowing your setup will enable you to decide what to bring.

Your New Roommate: Roommates are often assigned to those who live in dorms. Consider contacting them before starting so they won't be a total stranger when you finally meet. You could even coordinate who will bring shared items like audio equipment or coffee maker (ensure that your dorm allows such items).

Location: Knowing where your accommodation is situated can help you navigate campus efficiently. Be aware of the distance between your room and frequently visited places such as classes, dining hall, library, gym, etc. Check college maps and online maps like Google Earth for orientation.

Rules & Regulations: Every housing option has its own rules. Some dorms, for example, might not allow certain appliances for safety reasons. Off-campus housing might have restrictions regarding noise levels or guests. Knowing these rules can help manage your expectations and avoid potential issues.

Costs: Whether living in a dorm or off campus, be aware of rent or dorm costs, including deposits, when to pay, how often, payment methods, and what utilities are included, if any. Knowing these before arriving allows preparation to have funds to avoid paying late.

Prepare For Orientation

Orientation Week typically marks the start of the academic year and presents an excellent opportunity to learn about your new school, meet classmates, and get an overview of campus life. While the event itself is covered in greater depth in Chapter 3, it is essential to realize that making the most of this period will require planning.

Research Your College Orientation Events: Orientation programs last from a day to a week. Expect presentations on academics, housing, student services, and extracurricular activities. Check the schedule and register for events promptly.

Prepare Any Required Documents: Some colleges require placement tests and specific documents, like ID, health insurance proof, or financial aid forms. Review college communications to ensure you're prepared.

Take The Opportunity To Ask Questions: Think about and jot down any questions you have before the event. Also, contact current or recently graduated students for practical advice and insights to aid your preparation.

It's Not Only About Studying: Orientation is also about social aspects like clubs and organizations covering diverse areas such as academic interests, sports, arts, and more. Joining clubs is a great way to meet people, explore your hobbies, and discover new interests. Check the college website for information and contact clubs directly for more details. Some may require early application or audition.

Get Ready For Higher Education

Academic preparation ensures you have the skills, knowledge, and mindset to excel in your studies. Proactive preparation builds confidence and helps embrace learning opportunities.

Be familiar with your chosen courses and contact the academic advisors for more details. This will help you prepare mentally and even get a head start by brushing up on relevant topics if needed.

Gather essential supplies and materials needed for classes. These may include notebooks, pens, textbooks, a laptop, or other tools specific to your field of study. Being well-prepared will help you stay focused and engaged.

Develop time management skills. With classes, assignments, and extracurricular activities, it's easy to get overwhelmed. Managing time effectively is essential to meeting deadlines and keeping a healthy balance between academics and personal life. Chapter 4 offers valuable tips on smart and efficient studying, including effective time management techniques.

Finally, don't hesitate to seek help if you face any difficulties! Colleges usually have academic support services like tutoring centers or study groups where you can get assistance when needed. Don't be afraid to ask questions in class or approach your professors if you need clarification or guidance.

Banking

If you don't have a bank account, you must open one. A dedicated student bank account provides numerous benefits and is crucial in developing responsible financial habits. It is an essential tool to manage finances, from daily expenses to financial aid disbursements.

Why A Bank Account Is Important

A bank account allows you to take control of your finances and build a strong foundation for looking after your own money throughout your college years and beyond.

Convenience: A bank account makes it easy to deposit and withdraw money, pay bills, and manage your finances online or via mobile apps. This includes transferring money and checking your balance, which can be done 24/7 without visiting a bank branch.

Safety: Carrying large amounts of cash may be risky. A bank account is a more secure place to hold cash; plus, most banks protect your account in case of unauthorized transactions.

Direct Deposit: If you get a part-time job, many employers prefer to pay via direct deposit into a bank account. This method is faster, safer, and more convenient than receiving a physical check.

Building A Credit History: A bank account is often the first step towards getting a credit card, which helps build your credit history. For example, a good credit history will be necessary for apartment rentals, car loans, and mortgage applications later in life.

Develop Money Management Skills: A bank account allows you to track your balance, manage deposits and withdrawals, and ensure you have enough money for your needs. These are critical skills for managing your finances now and in the future.

Saving & Interest: Saving money is easier with a separate savings account. Over time, the funds in this account will earn interest, meaning your money will grow simply by being in the account. This can be a great way to put money aside for future expenditures and goals.

Which Bank Account?

When choosing a bank, look for student-friendly accounts with low or no fees, good online and mobile banking features, and conveniently located ATMs. Remember to understand any fees or requirements associated with the account, such as minimum balances or withdrawal limits. Don't hesitate to ask for clarification.

Many banks offer enticing incentives and benefits to attract you to open accounts with them. Some include fee waivers, overdraft protection, debit card rewards, and student credit cards.

Students need to research and compare the offerings of different banks to find the best fit for their needs. They should read reviews and ask fellow students about their experiences. Considering each bank's enticements and benefits allows for a more informed decision when choosing a student bank account.

Money Matters & Budgeting

As a student, you may juggle various expenses, from tuition fees and textbooks to housing, transportation, and social activities. It is easy to lose track of your spending, which can lead to financial challenges. That's where budgeting comes in.

Learn How To Budget Before Leaving For College: This will help you control your money and make informed decisions.

Financial Independence: College is usually the first time many students handle their finances. You'll likely have regular expenses, including food, personal care items, entertainment, and rent or housing costs. Budgeting helps manage expenses and live within means.

Avoiding Debt: Without a budget, it's easier to spend more money than you have and end up with unnecessary debt. This could result in bank overdraft fees, credit card debt, or even bigger student loans if you need more money to pay for expenses. A budget can keep you in check and help prevent spending money you don't have.

Less Stress: Money-related worries can harm your academic focus and well-being. A budget provides a clear financial picture and lowers stress.

Foster Responsibility: Budgeting encourages responsibility and accountability. It requires you to think about your spending habits and make conscious decisions.

Preparing For The Future: Budgeting is a crucial life skill. Learning this early helps you manage money better for post-college life.

Achieve Financial Goals: Whether saving for a spring break trip or paying off a student loan, a budget can help you get there.

Understanding the nuances of managing your money and budget early will help you settle into college life faster. It may take a few tries to get it right, but stay with it! Over time, budgeting will become second nature and significantly contribute to your financial health in college and beyond. For an in-depth discussion on specific finance and budgeting areas for students, head over to Chapter 11.

Health & Medical Needs

During your time at college, ensuring access to proper healthcare services and resources to maintain your well-being is essential.

Gather Medical Records & Relevant Health Information: This includes information about any chronic conditions you might have, allergies, vaccinations, and current medications. This readily available information will help healthcare providers offer you the best possible care if needed.

College Health Services: Most campuses have a student health center that provides medical attention for common illnesses, injuries, and routine check-ups. Note their hours and contact info beforehand for quick access if required.

Health Care Access: **Having healthcare access, whether** through your parents' or a college-provided insurance plan, will provide peace of mind should you need medical attention. Outside the US, healthcare requirements can vary; some countries have government healthcare programs, while others may require private insurance.

Common Illnesses: It is expected to fall ill, like with the 'Freshman Flu,' during the first weeks of college due to the proximity of dorm living and exposure to new germs. To minimize risk, avoid sharing personal items like drinking glasses and close contact with sick individuals. While this is a part of adjusting to campus life, students with chronic conditions or weaker immune systems should seek advice and guidance from their healthcare provider.

Visit Your Doctor: It is wise to schedule a doctor's appointment for advice and a pre-college check-up.

Meet Other Newbies Before Starting

Connecting with other incoming students before arrival can make the transition much smoother for various reasons, such as building your social network and having peers explore the new environment together. Remember, everyone else is probably as eager to meet new people as you are. Don't be afraid to introduce yourself and reach out to others before arriving at college.

Here are some ways to start connecting with your future classmates:

College Website / Social Media: Many colleges have web pages, webinars, or virtual meetups for incoming students. There are also official and unofficial groups for newcomers on platforms like Facebook and Instagram. Search for hashtags related to your college, courses, or class year.

Online College Forums: Websites such as CollegeConfidential.com and Reddit.com have forums where students discuss their experiences or ask questions.

Pre-College Summer Programs: Some colleges offer summer courses or orientation sessions to help students adjust to the college environment.

Academic Departments Or Clubs: If you've declared a major or are interested in a particular club, try reaching out to see if they can connect you with other incoming students with similar interests.

Develop Good Hygiene Habits

Emphasizing the importance of cultivating good hygiene habits is vital for college or life. The transition to college introduces new environments, more independence, and close interactions with fellow students. Good hygiene habits support overall health, build confidence, and leave a positive impression on others. They are essential for your well-being and the comfort of those around you and will facilitate a smoother transition into campus life. Below are some tips, even if they seem obvious or are already practiced by you.

Regular Bathing: Bathe or shower daily, especially after exercising.

Oral Hygiene: Teeth should be brushed twice and flossed daily. Regular dentist visits (typically every six months) are crucial for maintaining good oral health.

Hand Washing: Wash your hands often, especially before eating, after using the restroom, and being in public places. Carry hand sanitizer for situations when you can't wash your hands immediately.

Healthy Eating & Drinking: Your diet directly impacts bodily functions and smells. Eat a balanced diet and stay hydrated. Avoid excess consumption of odor-causing foods like garlic and onions if you're concerned about body or breath odor.

Deodorant/Antiperspirant: Apply daily to manage body odor. Select a product that matches your activity level and skin type.

Clean Clothes: Wash clothes regularly, especially socks and underwear. If you exercise or sweat a lot, change your clothes more often.

Bedding Hygiene: Wash your sheets and pillowcases at least every two weeks. Regularly changing your bedding can help prevent acne and other skin issues.

Avoid Placing Outside Items On Your Bed: Items such as shoes, bags, or outdoor clothing can carry dirt, allergens, and bacteria that may transfer to your bedding and skin. These items may also introduce unwanted odors or stains to your bedding, affecting the overall cleanliness of your sleeping environment.

Hair Care: The frequency of washing your hair depends on your hair type and preference, but try to keep it clean and well-groomed.

Nail Care: Keep these trimmed and clean, as long nails can harbor bacteria and germs.

It's important to remember that good hygiene habits vary from person to person, and what works for someone else may not work for you. It's a good idea to start practicing good hygiene habits as soon as possible, and you don't have to wait until college to do so!

Learn To Do Laundry!

Doing your own washing might seem daunting at first, but it can be a breeze with some helpful tips. These hacks will assist you in handling dirty clothes and improving your laundry routine. Familiarize yourself with these before heading to college. By mastering these laundry fundamentals, you'll be well-prepared for independent living. Remember that everyone experiences a laundry mishap at some point, so don't be too hard on yourself if you accidentally shrink a shirt or turn a load of laundry pink. It's all part of the learning process!

Sorting Washing: Separate your laundry into lights, darks, and whites to prevent colors from bleeding onto each other. Delicate items might also need to be washed separately to avoid damage.

Clothing Labels: Symbols provide instructions for properly washing, drying, and ironing clothes. Pay attention to recommended washing temperatures and drying methods to prevent shrinking, discoloration, or damage to your garments.

Using The Washing Machine & Dryer: Familiarize yourself with operating a washer and dryer, including detergent placement, selecting the correct settings, and loading and unloading your clothes.

Choosing The Right Detergent: Laundry cleaning agents come in various forms, such as liquid, powder, and single-dose pods. Some are tailored for specific garments, like delicates or dark colors. Those with sensitive skin should consider a fragrance-free and dye-free detergent.

Amount Of Detergent: Using the correct amount is crucial – too little will not clean your clothes properly, and too much can leave a residue. Follow the detergent's instructions as a guideline, adjusting as needed.

Consider Cold Water For Some Loads: Washing at this temperature effectively cleans while preserving color and garment longevity; it is also more environmentally friendly.

Treating Stains: Learn to promptly address common stains like food, ink, and sweat. Different stains require distinct treatments. Pre-soaking can help remove stubborn marks.

Hand Washing: Delicate items may require hand washing to prevent damage. Learn the correct technique to safeguard your clothing.

Drying: Not all clothing suits the dryer, so understanding how to air dry using hangers or drying racks is essential. This also saves on energy costs. Avoid over-drying or high heat settings, which can cause shrinkage or premature wear.

Folding & Storing Clothes: Proper folding or hanging clothes can help prevent wrinkles and maximize storage space once your laundry is clean and dry. Storing clothes properly will also increase their longevity.

Ironing: Knowing how to iron clothes is beneficial when a polished appearance is required, such as for interviews, work, or formal events.

Basic Cooking Skills

Even if you have a meal plan, preparing basic meals can come in handy when the dining hall is closed, you're burning the midnight oil with studies, or you crave a change from the usual options. Cooking skills improve with practice, so don't be discouraged by initial mistakes. Begin with these fundamentals and progressively explore new recipes as your confidence in the kitchen grows.

Pasta: This can be the foundation for countless meals. Know how to boil water, add the right amount of salt, and how long to cook pasta for to your desired level (typically "al dente"). From there, you can experiment with different sauces and add-ins.

Rice: This staple food pairs well with many dishes. Whether you have a rice cooker or a pot, it is a skill worth mastering. Microwavable steam cookers can cook rice perfectly in around 15 minutes.

Simple Stir-Fries: These are versatile and can be cooked quickly with nearly any combination of protein and veggies. Learn how to sauté or stir-fry vegetables and proteins (like chicken, tofu, or shrimp) and make a simple sauce from soy sauce, garlic, and other seasonings.

Eggs: These are a staple ingredient that can be cooked in many ways for any meal. Learn how to make scrambled eggs, boiled eggs, and omelets.

Grilled Cheese Sandwich & Soup: This is a classic combo and easy-to-make meal. You can add ham or turkey to the sandwich for extra protein and experiment with different types of cheese.

Baking Chicken Or Fish: Baking is a simple, healthy cooking method. It involves seasoning with herbs and spices, perhaps adding a little oil (not always necessary), then popping it in the oven.

Simple Salads: A good salad can serve as a main dish and is a great way to ensure you eat enough vegetables. Learn how to wash salad ingredients, chop various lettuce, and make a basic dressing. You can add chicken or beef for extra protein.

Pancakes or French Toast: Making a tasty breakfast can be a lifesaver for mornings when you're not rushed. Plus, these recipes typically require ingredients that are convenient to store.

Microwave Proficiency: Although not a recipe, understanding how to operate one is essential for its convenience and time-saving benefits. Learn to heat food evenly and prepare items like scrambled eggs or baked potatoes, making the most of this kitchen tool.

Knife Mastery: Familiarity with safe chopping, slicing, and dicing techniques not only speeds up cooking but also ensures kitchen safety. Hone your skills in cutting various produce items like onions, bell peppers, and tomatoes.

Staying In Touch with Home

When you're away at college, staying connected with your loved ones is important. Before departing, share your college contact details, such as email and mailing address, with your family and close friends. This way, they can contact you whenever they want to catch up or check on your well-being. Maintaining contact with your support network offers comfort and reassurance, especially during this significant period of change.

Determine the most effective ways to stay in touch with friends and family regularly. Numerous communication options exist, such as video chats, phone calls, texts, emails, or social media. Find the best methods for everyone and consider scheduling regular catch-up sessions. Keeping the lines of communication open will help you feel connected to home and your loved ones, even when you are miles away on campus.

While college can be exciting and busy, nurturing relationships with those who matter to you is equally important. Carving out time to talk to your family and friends can provide comfort and emotional support, helping you navigate any challenges or homesickness you may experience.

Tips For A Stress-Free Move

Moving to college can feel overwhelming, especially when figuring out what to pack and how to transport everything. Here are some suggestions to help smooth the process:

Plan Ahead: Start by listing all the things you will need. This will help avoid overpacking or forgetting essential items.

Consult Your College: Before packing, verify what your college or accommodation provides and what is permitted. For instance, check if desk lamps are included and what storage options are available.

Pack Strategically: Pack crucial items that will be needed immediately (e.g. a change of clothes, toiletries, medication, laptop, and important documents) in a separate bag or box. This ensures that the essentials are available to get you through the first few days, even if everything isn't unpacked immediately.

Smart Packing: Use vacuum-sealed bags for bulky items like bedding. Optimize space by storing socks or small items inside your shoes. Eliminate air gaps in your bags and safeguard fragile items by using bubble wrap or wrapping them inside clothing.

Label Boxes & Bags: Label each with a summary of their contents to simplify unpacking.

Hire A Moving Service Or Rent A Van: If you're moving far away or have a lot of belongings, consider using a moving service or hiring a van.

Packing Checklist

Start preparations early! Avoid leaving this to the last minute; make a checklist of items you need and start gathering them in advance. Keep in mind that these items enhance your experience, not clutter your space. If you're uncertain about an item, leave it behind and consider bringing it for the next semester. By then, you'll better understand your living space and needs. Below is a list of basic and practical items to pack. To download a printable copy of this checklist, scan the QR code towards the back of the book.

Basic Essentials

Clothing:

- Underwear and socks – a couple of weeks' worth is ideal.
- Pajamas / Nightwear.
- Casual clothes – tees, jeans, sweatshirts, etc.
- Exercise clothes and shoes if you plan to work out.
- Smart wear – for job interviews, internships, or formal occasions.
- Seasonal items – winter jackets, lighter summer clothing, raincoats.
- Shoes – casual, smart, athletic, plus flip-flops for the shower.

College Supplies & Tech:

- Backpack.
- Laptop and charger.
- Cellphone charger and cable.
- Notebooks, pens, pencils, highlighters, sticky notes, and binders.
- USB flash drive.
- Planner / Calendar – to manage time and keep track of deadlines.

Room Essentials:

- Bedding – sheets, comforter, pillow, and mattress pad.
- Towels – both for the shower and the hands.
- Shower caddy – to carry toiletries when sharing a communal bathroom.
- Small fan – in case your dorm room doesn't have AC, if permitted.
- Desk lamp and bedside reading light (check if already provided.)
- Power strip/extension lead – electric sockets for all your electronics.
- Mini fridge – if allowed and if you plan on keeping cold food/drinks.
- Storage solutions – including crates or under-bed storage boxes.
- Basic toolkit – handy to have as you never know when you'll need a screwdriver.

Kitchen Supplies:

- Water bottle.
- A couple of dishes, bowls, cups, and silverware.
- Few snacks – to get you started for when the dining hall is closed or you're studying late.
- Microwave – if permitted, and if not provided by your dorm.

Health:

- First aid kit – band-aids, ointment, etc.
- Over-the-counter medications – pain relievers, cold medicine, hay fever tablets, etc.
- Any prescription medications.
- Health insurance details.
- Glasses or contact lenses if applicable.
- Toiletries – personal care and hygiene items.

Miscellaneous:

- Key documents – driver's license, passport, social security card, etc.
- Decorations – photos, posters, and other items to make your room feel more like home.
- Banking – account details and bank cards.
- Laundry bag or basket and laundry detergent.

Remember, every college and dorm is different. Some items listed may not be needed, and items not listed may be necessary. Be sure to check with your college on what is provided and allowed in the dorm rooms.

Practical Items To Include

In addition to the above must-haves, there are other less obvious items that many students have found useful in college.

- Portable Charger and Spare Cell Battery – useful for those long days on campus when you cannot return to your dorm to recharge devices.
- White Noise Machine – helpful if you have loud roommates or live in a noisy dorm. It can provide soothing background noise that drowns out disruptions and enables better sleep.
- Earplugs – for noisy college dorms as a more affordable alternative to a White Noise Machine.
- Doorstop – great for dorm living as it keeps your door open, making

it more inviting for others to stop by and say hello.

- Drying Rack – is an alternative way to dry clothes without a dryer or if you want to save money on laundry.
- Reusable Shopping Bags – handy for carrying groceries or other items from the store to your dorm.
- Plants – they decorate your room and help to clean the air.
- Backrest Pillow – perfect for studying or working in bed.
- Safety Whistle – it's best to prioritize safety, particularly when walking around campus late at night.
- Long Charging Cables – electrical outlets might not be conveniently placed in a dorm; these longer cables ensure a phone or other devices can still be used comfortably while they charge.
- Sleep Mask – helps block out light, especially if your roommate likes to stay up later than you or your curtains let in a lot of light.
- Microwaveable Pasta or Rice – if a microwave is available, it can be a lifesaver if the dining hall is closed and you need a quick meal.
- Extra Storage Boxes – ottoman (also provides additional seating), hanging shelves.
- Over Door Organizer Hooks – great for coats, wet towels and bags.
- Padlock – secure items in lockers or for other lockable items.

Traveling To Campus

Transporting your belongings to college may be another issue that needs to be resolved. It can be complicated by luggage or space limitations and the challenge of transporting bulky items. Remember, less critical items can always be brought later. Traveling by private car would be the most flexible option in terms of comparatively more luggage space available. However, those journeying by public transport will face greater restrictions in terms of baggage. Here are some suggestions to ease the moving process:

Ship Items In Advance: This can be cost-effective for bulky or heavy items like bedding and books. Check with your college or landlord when they will accept student deliveries.

Buy On Arrival: Many basic items (such as toiletries) can be purchased in your college town. Many colleges have stores nearby, or online orders can be made and delivered to your new address.

Coordinate With Roommates: If you're sharing a living space, contact your roommates beforehand to decide who will bring shared items. If everyone is traveling from far away, consider splitting the cost of purchasing these items once you arrive.

Below are additional tips for those traveling by public transport to college.

Baggage Policy of Airline, Train, or Bus: Be aware of their rules on luggage size, weight restrictions, and any applicable fees for checked bags. This will help determine items to bring or buy upon arrival.

Carry Essentials In Hand Luggage: Include travel documents, medications, a change of clothes, toiletries (remember liquid restrictions, if applicable), and valuables. Luggage can go missing, so having the most critical items with you is crucial.

Arrange Onward Transportation: Plan how to travel from the airport, train station, or bus terminal to college. Some colleges offer shuttle services, or you can use public transport, a taxi, or a ride-sharing service.

Timetable To Help Plan Your Move

This final section provides a simple timetable to help you plan key tasks before leaving for college. Start early to allow you enough time to organize and plan. Use the provided tips and lists as guidance, and remember that flexibility is key - ultimately, you decide what suits you best. To download a printable copy of this timetable, scan the QR code towards the back of the book.

3 Months Before Departure

- Start a checklist of what will be needed in college.
- Find out what is recommended to bring and what is provided.
- Begin sorting through belongings to decide what to bring.
- Research part-time jobs if planning to work while at college.
- Plan your transportation to college: if flying, book tickets; if driving, check and maintain your car's condition.

2 Months Before Departure

- Purchase necessary items e.g. bedding, toiletries, clothing.
- Contact roommates on bringing shared items to avoid duplication.
- Organize health insurance if needed.
- Open a bank account if you haven't already.
- Check to ensure vital documents, such as identification and insurance, are valid and up to date.

1 Month Before Departure

- Confirm the move-in date and times with your college.
- Check your health: Get necessary vaccinations, eye exams, and dental check-ups, and gather necessary prescription medications.
- Pack non-essentials that are not needed in the last weeks at home.
- Ensure your cell phone plan is adequate while at college.

2 Weeks Before Departure

- Pack most of your belongings except for still needed essentials.
- If not on a meal plan, shop for non-perishable food items if luggage space allows.
- Pack essential documents in your hand luggage.
- Confirm your transportation plans. If driving, plan the route and rest stops. If by public transport, double-check luggage restrictions.

1 Week Before Departure

- Pack essential items.
- Double-check that all essential documents are in your possession.
- Say goodbye to local friends and family; plan how to stay in touch.

Day Before Departure

- Do a final check; ensure nothing needed is left unpacked.
- Try to relax and get a good night's sleep. You have a big day ahead!

Preparing properly before leaving home is crucial as you embark on your new life at college. The steps you take now will lay a solid foundation for your college experience. Taking the time to organize, plan, and understand what lies ahead will make your transition smoother and less daunting. Remember, college is not just about academic growth but also personal development, making new friends, and exploring new horizons. You give yourself the best possible start by ensuring you're well-prepared. It's natural to feel excitement and nervousness, but with proper preparation, you increase the chances for success and for all to go smoothly. Embrace what lies ahead, knowing you've done your best to prepare for this major change in your life.

Chapter 2

From Chaos To Comfort: Unpacking & Settling In

" Change is the only constant in life. One's ability to adapt to those changes will determine your success in life."

Benjamin Franklin

Stepping onto a college campus as a newbie can feel both scary and exciting. Your first task is to turn an empty room into your home. Make the most of limited space and add a personal touch to every corner. Each unpacked box brings you closer to calling this place home.

Organizing Your New Home

Unpacking Tips

Moving into a new college accommodation marks the beginning of your college experience. But before settling in, unpacking and organizing your belongings is essential to turning your new living area into a comfortable sanctuary. Creating your own organized space will help you feel more settled and promote a favorable environment for studying, socializing and relaxation.

Effective Unpacking: Start by bringing out the immediate essentials, such as bedding, toiletries, and a few changes of clothes. As you unpack, sort items into categories, making it easier to find what you need later. Then, organize your belongings to match your lifestyle and preferences.

Room Layout & Furniture Arrangement: First, consider the optimal layout for your room; pay attention to the flow of the space and arrange the furniture accordingly. If possible, try different configurations to determine the one that optimizes space and functionality for you.

Declutter & Minimize: It is important to minimize unnecessary items due to limited space, and a clutter-free environment will create a sense of openness. Hopefully, you will only have brought items that serve a purpose or hold sentimental value.

Storage Solutions: Utilize under-bed storage bins, hanging organizers, and stackable containers to maximize every inch of available space. Organize your room with designated storage areas for items to maintain order and easy access.

Personalize Your Space: Add A Touch of You

Your college accommodation is more than just a place to sleep; it reflects your personality and allows you to express yourself fully. After unpacking, it is time to add your personal touch: consider decorating your room with posters, photographs, or artwork that resonates with you. Display items that bring comfort or remind you of home, such as a favorite blanket or cherished keepsakes. Always check with your college or landlord first on what is permitted before decorating your room.

Color & Décor: A carefully chosen color scheme can impact the mood of your space. Choose colors that evoke positive emotions. Whether you love vibrant hues or calming neutrals, the color scheme sets the tone of your space. Integrate decorative elements like throw pillows and rugs that complement the colors and add personality to your room.

Happy Memories: Incorporate items that hold special memories or represent significant moments in your life. Displaying photographs with friends, family, or cherished experiences is a constant reminder of the people and moments that matter most.

Plants & Greenery: Incorporate greenery to add life to your living space. Houseplants enhance the ambiance and provide various health benefits, such as improving air quality and lowering stress. Choose low-maintenance plants that suit your room's lighting conditions.

Showcase Hobbies & Interests: Whether it's displaying musical instruments, sports memorabilia, or your favorite books, integrating these will make the space feel uniquely yours.

Functional Storage: Opt for storage solutions that align with your décor style. Organize belongings by investing in appropriate storage bins, shelves, and organizers.

Lighting Accents: Experiment with lighting to create different moods in your room. String or unique lights can add a warm and cozy ambiance. Adjustable lighting options can also create the perfect study environment or a relaxing atmosphere for winding down.

Create A Productive Study Area

Studying and academic success are major parts of college life, and a dedicated and productive study area is therefore essential. But it is more than just a desk and a chair; it is about curating an environment that nurtures your academic pursuits and supports your learning process. While you may be restricted to the dorm space available, you can still create a well-designed study space within these limitations.

Location Matters: Choose an area separate from your bed and other distractions. This will help associate the space with studying and maintain a clear boundary between work and relaxation. If possible, position the study area near a window for natural light.

Ergonomics: If feasible, invest in a comfortable chair and a good-sized desk of appropriate height. This will reduce physical strain during study sessions and enhance overall comfort.

Organized Desk: Keep your desk area clutter-free and well-organized; have designated places for pens, laptops, and study materials. Use desk organizers or drawers to keep essential items easily accessible.

Inspirational Elements: Display motivational items that inspire you. Hang up inspirational quotes, pictures of role models, or a vision board representing your goals and aspirations.

Greenery: Plants or fresh flowers can help create a calming and inviting atmosphere and bring a touch of nature to your room.

Noise Management: In a shared living environment, noise can be challenging. Invest in earplugs or noise-canceling headphones to block out distractions when needed. Alternatively, play instrumental music or white noise to create a study-conducive environment.

Study Break Area: Designate a nearby area for breaks from studying. It can be a cozy reading nook, a comfortable chair, or a space to stretch and move around. Taking regular breaks is crucial to maintain focus and prevent burnout.

Tech-Savvy Living: Utilize Smart Technology

In today's digital age, technology has become an integral part of our lives, and harnessing its power can transform your space into a more efficient environment and boost productivity. However, finding a balance and avoiding over-reliance on technology is essential, ensuring it remains a place of comfort and creativity.

Smart Lighting: Install smart bulbs that can be controlled through your smartphone or voice commands. Adjust the brightness and color temperature to suit different activities, such as bright white for studying or warm ambient lighting for relaxation.

Voice Assistants: Consider adding these to your space; they can answer questions, set reminders, play music, and control smart devices in your room through voice commands.

Digital Organizers & Cloud Storage: Productivity apps and note-taking tools facilitate digital organization. Keep track of schedules, assignments, and deadlines on your smartphone or computer. Online cloud storage providers ensure files are accessible from any device.

Safety First Always

It is common to get caught up in the excitement of college life. Still, it is essential not to overlook the crucial aspect of personal safety and emergency preparedness. Every student must take the necessary steps to ensure their safety, whether by securing their rooms, being aware of their surroundings, or knowing how to react in unexpected situations. Personal safety goes beyond just protecting oneself physically; it also involves safeguarding personal belongings and preventing situations that may jeopardize one's safety and security.

Campus Safety Resources: Take the time to become familiar with the safety resources available on the college campus. This may include emergency alert systems, campus security, and evacuation points. Understand the procedures for different emergencies, such as severe weather or fires.

Locking Doors & Windows: Always lock up when you leave your room or apartment, even if only for a few minutes. It's also good to keep them locked at night.

Emergency Exits & Routes: Learn where these are and familiarize yourself with the quickest way to get out in an emergency. Knowing at least two routes out of the neighborhood is also a good idea.

Lighting: A well-lit living space can deter potential intruders. Ensure there is sufficient outdoor lighting, especially near entrances. If living off-campus, ask your landlord to address any outdoor lighting issues.

Create An Emergency Kit: This should comprise essential items, including a flashlight, extra batteries, a first aid kit, non-perishable food, water, and a portable phone charger. Keep this kit readily accessible in case of emergencies.

ICE Contacts: Save key "In Case of Emergency" ("ICE") contact numbers on your phone and keep an easily accessible written copy. This list should include campus security, local police, medical services, and personal emergency contacts.

Fire Safety: Familiarize yourself with the fire safety protocols in your residence: know the locations of fire exits, extinguishers, and fire alarm pull stations. Avoid using prohibited appliances or overloading electrical outlets, and never leave cooking unattended. Ensure there are working smoke detectors that are regularly tested.

Securing Valuables: Keep precious items out of sight and in a secure location. Consider insurance to cover your personal property in case of theft or damage.

Personal Safety Behavior: Be mindful of your safety on and off campus. Avoid walking by yourself at night in unfamiliar or poorly lit areas. Use well-lit paths and travel with a friend or in a group whenever possible. Always trust your instincts and report suspicious activity to campus authorities or local law enforcement. If something doesn't feel right, it probably isn't.

Campus Safety Escorts: Some college campuses offer this service to students who may feel unsafe walking alone at night. Take advantage of this, especially when walking in poorly lit or secluded areas on campus.

Underage Drinking & Substance Use: In the US, the minimum drinking age is 21, so consuming alcohol below this age is illegal. If you still choose to drink despite this, do so responsibly and be aware of your limits. Never leave your drink unattended, and look out for your friend's well-being. Avoid substance use and be cautious of accepting drinks or substances from strangers.

Online Safety: Practice safe online habits to protect personal information and privacy. Be cautious about sharing sensitive information or engaging in risky online behaviors. Use strong, unique passwords for your accounts, and be vigilant of phishing attempts or suspicious links. Also, be careful about what you post on social media. Sharing that you are out of town or posting photos revealing you live alone can attract unwanted attention.

Identity Safety: Shred documents containing personal information before discarding them. Be cautious when giving out your address or other personal information.

Know Your Neighbors: Try to meet the people living around you. They can be a valuable resource in keeping an eye on your property when you're away, and you can do the same for them.

Stay Informed: Stay up to date with campus safety notifications and local news. Follow official college communication channels to stay informed about potential risks or safety precautions.

Your Campus & Beyond

Knowing the surrounding area, whether you live on or off campus, is important. Being familiar with the area helps you feel more connected, ultimately making it easier to settle in confidently and comfortably.

Campus Familiarity: Your college is more than just a place to attend lectures; it is a vibrant community with resources that are often underutilized. Find key locations such as the library, study rooms, gym, health center, and dining facilities. Check out on-site convenience stores and note their opening hours for those late-night study snack cravings.

Take note of the location of security offices and save the campus security contact on your phone. Understanding where these are located and how to use them provides security and reassurance.

Going Off-Site: Exploring beyond the campus is equally important. Look for the nearest grocery stores, pharmacies, restaurants, and other essential services. Knowing these provides a wider choice and can help reduce stress when the needs arise.

Local Transport: Knowing which bus routes or subway lines to take can help you navigate the city more efficiently.

Understanding Your Neighborhood: If living off-campus, get to know your community. Take note of the general atmosphere during the day and at night. Knowing the usual patterns can help you identify when something seems off or out of place. This can be crucial for your safety. Try to meet your neighbors as they can provide valuable insights about the neighborhood and look out for you.

Connecting With Nature: Most campuses have green or open spaces, which can be great places to relax, exercise, or socialize with friends.

Off-Campus Living

While the primary focus is on settling in and getting to know your new living space, it would be an oversight to exclude new students who have chosen to live off-campus. With the freedom from non-campus housing comes new responsibilities, such as lease agreements, tenant obligations, and renter's insurance. Understanding these and being aware of tenant's rights will enable a smoother integration into your new living space and minimize any potential uncertainties or stress that may arise.

Understanding Lease Agreements

This is a legal contract between the tenant (you) and the landlord. This document will outline terms such as the length of the lease, the monthly rent, the due date for payments, and the rules you are required to follow as a tenant. The lease might also specify what the landlord is responsible for, such as maintenance and repairs.

Before signing a lease, ensure you fully understand what you agree to. It is crucial to know the length of the lease term, typically 12 months, and whether it aligns with your academic schedule. If you're only attending school for 9 months out of the year, consider negotiating a shorter lease or find out about subletting options.

Look for clauses in the lease on renewals, late fees, and security deposits. Be aware of policies on pets, roommates, and changes to the apartment. It is also essential to know what conditions could lead to eviction.

Your Obligation As Tenant

Living off-campus comes with obligations you may not have experienced in a dorm. Besides rent, you may also be responsible for utilities, such as electricity, water, gas, internet, and trash collection. Ensure you understand which you're responsible for and how and when to pay them.

A tenant is also obligated to maintain the rental property. While the landlord is generally responsible for major repairs and maintenance, tenants must keep the place clean, dispose of trash properly, and promptly report any damage or necessary repairs to the landlord.

Also, be respectful of your neighbors. Noise or behavior that disturbs others could lead to complaints to the landlord or even the police.

Renter's Insurance

This insurance policy protects renters against losses due to theft, fire, or other damages. Additionally, it can provide liability coverage if someone is injured in your rental unit. Many students overlook this important aspect of renting, but it can be a financial lifesaver in case of unexpected events.

Consider what it would cost to replace your possessions if they were stolen or damaged. That could include personal items like clothes, electronics, and furniture brought into the rental. It is a good idea to take an inventory of belongings and consider their total value before deciding whether to buy renter's insurance.

Know Your Rights

Renters have rights protected by law, and it is crucial to know what these are. While these rights can vary from state to state or country to country, some general principles apply to most rental situations.

Disclaimer: The information provided regarding off-campus student rentals, including but not limited to obligations, insurance, and tenant rights, serves as a basic guideline only and is intended for general informational purposes. It does not constitute professional or legal advice. Every rental situation may be unique, and laws can vary by jurisdiction. It is the renter's responsibility to understand the terms of any rental agreement. It is strongly recommended to seek advice from a qualified expert or an authorized legal professional.

Unpacking and settling in is the first step towards creating a comfortable and personalized living space. By organizing your belongings efficiently and decorating your room to reflect your personality, you create an environment conducive to both relaxation and study. Whether arranging furniture to maximize space, minimizing clutter, or adding personal touches with decor, these efforts make your room feel like home. Furthermore, establishing a productive study area and embracing smart technology can significantly enhance your living and learning experience.

Remember, safety must always be a priority - familiarize yourself with campus safety resources and maintain good practices to secure your belongings and personal safety. Lastly, getting to know your surroundings on and off campus will help you settle in more confidently and comfortably. Now that your home base is established, you're all set to dive into college life!

CHAPTER 3
IT'S ORIENTATION WEEK!

" Twenty years from now you will be more disappointed by the things that you didn't do than by the ones you did do."

Mark Twain

Starting college is a big deal and having a clear direction, a defined plan, and an openness to exploring the unknown is essential. This pivotal week is designed to ease your transition into college life. It comprises informative tours, sessions, and workshops that allow you to explore the campus, its resources, and the community. It's also filled with social events that allow you to meet fellow students and immerse yourself in the vibrant culture of your college.

For simplicity, "Orientation Week" will be the collective term used to describe what may also be known as "Welcome Week," "Fresher's Week," or "First Week of School." This chapter covers what can be expected during this first week and encourages you to take full advantage of this opportunity.

Orientation Week & SOAR

Orientation Week: Often referred to as "O Week," is a dynamic and immersive introduction to college life designed to welcome new students with open arms. This period typically takes place just before the start of the academic year and serves as a comprehensive introduction to campus culture. During O Week, there is the opportunity to become familiar with the campus layout, discover essential resources such as support services, and engage in many varied activities. It might include campus tours, icebreaker activities, seminars about academic expectations, and social events. O Week is much more than a series of events; it is a bridge between high school and college, a gateway to forming connections, building a support network, and finding your footing in this new environment.

Student Orientation, Advising, & Registration: Often referred to as "SOAR," this is a program run by some colleges that goes hand in hand with O Week. SOAR takes O Week a step further by not only introducing you to campus life but also ensuring a smooth academic transition. It includes academic advisory sessions to clarify degree requirements, choose the suitable courses for your major, and map out your academic journey. SOAR often culminates in registration for the first semester's classes and ensures you are on track from the start.

O Week & SOAR Unified As "Orientation Week"

Not all colleges have separate events for O Week and SOAR; some may combine them. However, due to their shared goal of assisting first-year students, both events will be considered together in this book and collectively referred to as "Orientation Week." Remember that whether you are partaking in Orientation Week, SOAR, or both, the goal is to ensure your college journey starts with enthusiasm, knowledge, and a strong sense of belonging.

Whether you are an introvert apprehensive about a crowd, an extrovert raring to dive into the social whirlpool, or a serious academic ready to hit the books, Orientation Week has something for everyone. Embracing the opportunities, being open to new experiences, and remembering how you approach Orientation Week could set the tone for the rest of your college life.

A Must-Attend ....Or Not?

Orientation Week is an optional extracurricular activity. However, it is an invaluable part of transitioning into college life, a well-rounded launchpad for students beginning their higher education journey. So, it's a definite YES to attend! Here are some reasons why every student should participate.

Information Gathering

Acclimatization To New Environment: Moving to a new place can be overwhelming, even more so when it is an educational institution that will be your home for several years. Orientation Week helps students familiarize themselves with the campus layout, facilities, and services. Knowing where essential resources are can ease initial anxiety.

Academic Preparation: Programs and sessions about academic expectations, registration processes, and course selection are usually available. Learning about these can help prevent common mistakes and set you on the correct educational path.

Networking: This period is one of the best opportunities to meet a broad spectrum of individuals, including fellow students, faculty members, and administrative staff. Students form connections and friendships through various social events, team-building activities, and group sessions. The shared experience of being new to college can bond students, creating a sense of community that can make the college experience less daunting.

Cultural Transition: For international students or those from different cultural backgrounds, Orientation Week can be a helpful introduction to the college's cultural norms and expectations. These may include understanding a new education system, practicing a new language, or simply adapting to a new way of life.

Extracurricular Pursuits: Colleges usually offer a diverse range of clubs, organizations, and non-academic activities. You can learn about these offerings and how to get involved during this time. Participation in these contributes to a well-rounded education and can enrich your college experience.

Resources & Support Services: Many students aren't initially aware of the breadth of support services available, including mental health resources, tutoring services, career advice, and financial aid offices. Orientation Week often includes introductions to these areas, enabling students to utilize them fully when needed.

Personal Development

There are also intangible and more subtle but important reasons why you should consider attending Orientation Week. These relate to self-development and making the most of this time in your life.

New Horizons: College life provides the chance to explore and embrace new experiences. It is a time to savor the richness of diversity and discover aspects of yourself you never knew existed. Trying new activities allows you to broaden your horizons, cultivate a sense of adventure, and build invaluable life skills.

Exploring new opportunities, such as joining an unfamiliar club or enrolling in a course unrelated to your major, can lead to personal growth and self-development. Embrace the excitement of the unknown, as these experiences can boost your confidence and prepare you for life's challenges with an open-minded approach.

Be Brave: Taking on new experiences can be intimidating, but being open to trying something unfamiliar can lead to new interests and adventures. College is a nurturing environment where you can shed inhibitions, push boundaries, and develop resilience. Whether engaging in public speaking or attempting a new sport, remember that every "first time" is an opportunity for growth. Being brave means accepting that failure may happen, but these experiences will make you more determined and adaptable. Seize the chance to challenge your preconceptions and discover hidden talents!

Carpe Diem! College is a melting pot of opportunities where many experiences await. It is a time when almost everything you could dream of trying is conveniently within reach. From academic pursuits to extracurricular activities, campus life offers activities that cater to diverse interests and passions. The beauty of this all-in-one access is that it facilitates exploration without constraints, making it easier than ever to sample a wide range of experiences. Whether you have an appetite for the arts, sciences, or entrepreneurship, college provides the perfect platform to savor these opportunities fully. After university, the chances of having so many different opportunities so conveniently located fall dramatically, and it becomes harder to seek new experiences. Therefore, make the most of this unique time when the world is at your fingertips and yours to explore. Be open-minded and try something new. Cherish the freedom to experiment, as this period of your life won't last forever.

What To Uncover During Orientation Week

Orientation Week is designed to provide a wealth of information and support and allows you to acclimatize to the new environment before the pressure of classes begins. During this period, new college students should make sure to learn about some important aspects of college life, such as:

Campus Facilities & Services: Familiarize yourself with the campus layout, including academic buildings, libraries, student centers, health services, counseling centers, dining facilities, and recreational areas. Organized campus tours would be a great way to explore your new surroundings.

Academic Advising & Course Registration: This is a crucial step! Attend sessions to understand degree requirements, plan your schedule, and receive advice on the best classes for your major or interests. Academic advisors can offer insights into program requirements and guide you through selecting courses that align with your goals.

Registration Dates & Deadlines: Understanding these crucial dates allows you to plan and secure the desired courses and avoid missing out on essential classes.

College Policies & Procedures: Understanding the academic code of conduct, grading policies, and other important regulations will facilitate your learning. Appreciating these policies early on sets the groundwork for responsible and successful academic pursuits.

Student Support Services: During Orientation Week, students are introduced to various services that provide academic and personal support. These services include tutoring centers and career guidance to ensure students' success and well-being. Familiarizing yourself with these resources early on will better equip you to seek academic assistance. Moreover, you can manage stress and seek guidance during challenging times by discovering your campus's mental health support services.

Student Organizations & Clubs: These groups offer diverse interests and passions, from academic pursuits to hobbies and social causes, and can enrich your college experience. Exploring these options allows you to find like-minded individuals who share your interests and create lasting friendships. These organizations aren't just clubs; they are communities that foster personal growth, leadership skills, and friendships.

Health & Safety: Prioritize your well-being by uncovering the health and safety resources available on campus should the need arise.

Housing & Residential Life: If living on campus, learn about the dorm or residence hall rules and the resources provided by the residential life office. Acquainting yourself with these will help you to settle in more easily.

Financial Aid & Tuition: Understand your financial aid package, tuition payment options, available scholarships, and deadlines for submitting required documents. Being aware of the resources provided by your college's financial aid office can help you make informed decisions about funding your education and managing your finances.

Technology Services: To better prepare for accessing online resources, learn about the college's technology setup, including email systems, online platforms, and campus Wi-Fi.

Transportation: Learn how to get around on and off campus, such as shuttle services, public transportation, and parking permits. This will allow you to easily explore the city or town of your college, attend off-campus events, and ensure efficient movement between classes and activities.

College Events & Traditions: Learn about gatherings, celebrations, and time-honored rituals. These can be fun and meaningful activities that happen every year. Discover the cool traditions that make your college unique. Getting involved in these events is also a great way to make friends and be part of the college spirit.

Library Resources: Familiarize yourself with the library facilities, databases, physical collections, and research support available to enhance your academic work. This will enable you to navigate research projects and assignments effectively.

Research & Internship Opportunities: Inquire about research opportunities, internships, and career-related programs that can complement your academic studies. Orientation Week opens the door to potential collaborations with professors and connections with industries beyond the campus. By exploring these avenues, you can apply classroom knowledge to real-world scenarios, gain practical experience, and enhance your resume.

Academic Support Workshops: Attend workshops or seminars for strategies on time management, study skills, and academic success. These sessions provide insights into effective note-taking, exam preparation, and time-efficient study habits.

Embracing Diversity & Celebrating Differences

One of the defining aspects of college life is the incredible diversity you will encounter. College campuses often bring together individuals of diverse cultures, backgrounds, ideologies, life experiences, and perspectives. When you engage with people different from you, whether in terms of nationality, race, religion, socioeconomic status, gender, or sexual orientation, you can better see the world through different lenses. This can challenge pre-existing beliefs, stimulate intellectual curiosity, and foster empathy - qualities that are not only invaluable for your personal growth but also vital in today's increasingly interconnected world.

During Orientation Week, you will likely meet students from around the globe, each with unique perspectives and experiences. Engage with them, be open to their stories, and share yours. Engaging in such exchanges broadens your understanding of the world and helps develop empathy, openness, and a greater sense of global citizenship.

Some resources promote and support diversity, such as multicultural centers, LGBTQ+ resources, and international student organizations. Do utilize them, whether or not you are part of these communities, as they provide a welcoming, inclusive environment for all students.

Remember that diversity is one of the greatest strengths of a college campus. In this diverse community, you will learn not just from textbooks and lectures but also from your peers' rich, varied experiences and perspectives. Understanding and appreciating diversity will enhance your college experience and prepare you for a globalized world where cultural competency is highly valued.

Breaking The Ice: How To Make New Connections

Orientation Week is an excellent opportunity to start building solid relationships with your roommate, hallmates, or neighbors. No matter your personality, preferences, or apprehensions, these early connections can contribute to a positive living environment and provide a supportive network throughout college.

Sharing living quarters with someone new, especially in a setting as unique as a college dorm, is not just about cohabitation but social integration, adaptation, and communication. It is about sharing a part of your life with someone who was once a stranger but may become a lifelong friend.

Many students will likely feel nervous during Orientation Week, so be patient, understanding, and kind. The goal is not to become best friends immediately but to lay the foundation for a respectful and positive living situation. Over time, these connections may evolve into lasting friendships. But for now, focus on cultivating a comfortable and supportive relationship.

Participate In Activities Together: Orientation Week is filled with activities designed to help break the ice and help students get to know each other. Team-building exercises, group discussions, or a simple campus tour with your roommate or hallmate can foster a shared sense of adventure and camaraderie.

Shared Meals: Eating together is a universal bonding experience. Shared meals provide an informal, relaxed setting for conversing and learning about each other's backgrounds, interests, and habits.

Initiate Conversations: Be proactive when starting conversations. Ask about the other person's hometown, hobbies, or why they chose the college. Show genuine interest and listen actively. Sharing personal stories helps create a bond and helps people understand each other better.

Respect Boundaries: As much as it is important to be friendly, respecting each other's personal space and boundaries is equally crucial. Some might take a little longer to open up, which is perfectly okay.

Establish Common Ground: Identifying shared interests can help break the ice. It could be a favorite movie genre, a shared passion for a particular sport, or mutual academic interests.

Offer To Help: Whether figuring out a class schedule or locating a building, helping can demonstrate goodwill and foster mutual respect.

Set Expectations: Discuss living arrangements with your roommate in the early days. Talk about sleep schedules, study habits, cleaning responsibilities, guest policies, etc. Clear discussions from the beginning can prevent misunderstandings and conflicts later.

How To Conquer Shyness

Not everyone arriving on campus is brimming with confidence, ready to take on new experiences with enthusiasm. You may feel shy, reserved, and timid, and the prospect of Orientation Week may induce a wave of anxiety. In fact, for many, stepping onto a college campus for the first time can feel like landing on a different planet. Everything is new and a little intimidating. This feeling can be even more intense for those naturally introverted or shy.

As you approach Orientation Week, you might wonder how to navigate the bustling crowds, the flood of unfamiliar faces, and the ceaseless flow of social interaction. Fear not, because there are simple, practical tips on overcoming shyness or reservations in the earlier days of college. This is not about changing who you are but providing the tools to express yourself and connect with others.

Prepare In Advance: Before orientation begins, be familiar with your campus's schedule and layout. Knowing where to go and what to expect can help reduce anxiety.

Set Realistic Goals: Plan for small, achievable goals for each day. This could be as simple as starting a conversation with one new person, asking a question during a session, or attending a social event.

Use Icebreakers: Come up with a list of simple, open-ended questions you can ask new acquaintances to help initiate conversations. Examples of these could be:

"Where are you from?"

"Have you found any exciting clubs or organizations on campus to join?

"What is your major? What drew you to that field of study?"

"What is the last book you read or movie you watched that you enjoyed?"

"What are you most excited about for this upcoming year?"

"Which classes are you considering?"

"What is the most interesting class you've signed up for this semester (and why)?"

"What is one place you want to travel to in the future?"

"What do you like to do to destress or relax?"

"Have you found any cool spots on campus yet?"

"Do you have any favorite music artists? I'm always looking for new music recommendations!"

Remember, the goal of these icebreakers is not just to start a conversation but to find common ground and create a connection with the person you're talking to. Listen carefully to their answers and share your own experiences or interests in return. This exchange can help you both feel more comfortable and foster a meaningful conversation.

Seek Out Smaller Groups: Large crowds can be overwhelming. Find smaller groups or one-on-one situations where you feel more comfortable expressing yourself.

Use A Doorstop To Keep Your Door Open: An open door is more friendly and inviting than a closed one, making it easier for people to drop in.

Participate In Activities You Enjoy: This can be particularly helpful for naturally more reserved people. Meeting people who share your enthusiasm can lead to meaningful friendships as you bond over your mutual passion, whether sports, music, or gaming.

Practice Active Listening: If speaking makes you nervous, remember that being a good listener is just as important in a conversation. Express genuine interest in what others say and respond with kindness and understanding.

Seek Support: Contact the orientation leaders or counselors if you need more support. They are there to provide advice.

Everyone Is In The Same Boat: Remember you are not alone; many may feel as nervous as you. Knowing you're not the only one can be comforting and make initiating conversations easier.

Be Patient With Yourself: It is okay to feel shy or nervous! Don't put pressure on yourself - change takes time, and there is no rush.

Overcoming shyness or reservations is a journey, not a race. While Orientation Week is an excellent time to start, remember that everyone's progress is unique, and there is no one-size-fits-all timeline. Your college experience is just beginning, and there is plenty of time to find your footing. With time, you'll find your comfort zone and form connections that can last a lifetime.

Nurturing New Friendships in the First Semester

Orientation Week can be frantic when everyone tries especially hard to make new friends and try new experiences. But as the semester formally starts and students begin to settle into their routines, how can new friendships be nurtured?

Plan An Outing: Organize a casual outing with a roommate or new acquaintance at a nearby attraction or event on campus. This will help everyone relax and interact in a non-academic, fun environment.

Create A Hallmate Group Chat: If your residence hall doesn't already have one, create a group chat for those in your dorm. This can be a great place to plan activities, share information, and engage in light-hearted conversations.

Decorate Your Common Space Together: If you share a common area, decorating it together can be a great bonding activity. It can help you understand each other's tastes and preferences and foster a sense of shared responsibility.

Participate In Hall Meetings: Attend meetings or activities planned by your residence advisor. These gatherings often include ice-breaking activities and can be an excellent way to interact with your hallmates.

Engage In Friendly Competition: If a game room in your residence or a sports event is happening, invite your new friends for a friendly match. It can be fun to bond and learn more about each other.

Ask Their Opinion Or Advice: This demonstrates that you value their opinions, which can lead to more meaningful discussions.

Show Empathy: Moving to college is a significant transition that can bring a mix of excitement and anxiety. Show understanding to your new friends who may be experiencing homesickness or feeling overwhelmed.

Share A Hobby: If you have a pastime that can be shared, such as watching movies or cooking, invite your friends to join in. This can be an excellent opportunity for bonding and creating shared memories.

Building and maintaining friendships requires time and effort, so don't get discouraged if you don't connect with everyone immediately. Avoid comparing your experiences with others, as everyone's journey is unique. Stay open, positive, and patient. With time and shared experiences, you'll likely discover common ground and create lasting connections that can carry you through your college years and beyond.

Once Orientation Week has wrapped up, you'll be equipped with the essentials: a lay of the land, a clear sense of available resources, and the beginnings of friendships and a social network. With this foundation, you are ready to transition from a newcomer to an engaged student.

As the routines of college life begin to set in, it's important to maintain the spirit of engagement and the proactive stance adopted during Orientation Week. Remember, the success of your college experience lies not only in classrooms and textbooks but also in everyday interactions and your immersion into campus life. Use the confidence and knowledge gained during Orientation Week to move forward, and don't hesitate to reach out to new connections or support services.

With a full academic and social calendar ahead, you are well-prepared to make the most of this pivotal time in your life. Take charge and make it happen!

CHAPTER 4

STUDY SMARTER, NOT HARDER

" Tell me and I forget. Teach me and I remember.
Involve me and I learn."

Benjamin Franklin

Smart Studying For The Modern Student

The learning environment in college differs significantly from high school. Unlike the more structured setting with greater teacher oversight in high school, college students must take a more independent approach to their work. The teaching pace is faster, the content is more complex, and effective study strategies and time management become crucial. This is known as "Smart Studying," which goes beyond mere hours spent at the desk; it's about effectively managing time and studying.

Smart studying is an approach tailored to a student's busy life, and this chapter delves into practical ways to achieve it. In addition to basic practices, advanced techniques are provided for those seeking to elevate their study game to the next level. While the methods may only suit some individuals, some will hopefully introduce new ways of learning.

Understand Course & Study Requirements

College is not just about memorizing facts or passing exams. It is about developing a deep understanding of the subjects and building skills that will be useful in the future. Having clear expectations helps students to focus effectively and avoid wasting time on less important areas.

At the start of a course, it is crucial to know the syllabus, assignments, and grading criteria which outline the topics to be covered and how work will be evaluated. Review these materials thoroughly and refer to them regularly to ensure study efforts remain aligned with course goals.

Build a Rapport With Academic Staff

Connecting with professors and academic staff is often neglected by students. This is not about favoritism or special attention but building a meaningful educational relationship. Academic staff are a source of knowledge and can provide guidance, feedback, and support.

Start by participating in class, asking thoughtful questions and contributing to discussions. This not only helps them recognize you but also enriches your learning experience. Additionally, office hours can be an opportunity to seek advice and discuss coursework.

Having a good relationship with academic staff can deliver many benefits. In addition to personalized guidance and feedback, they can often provide career advice and write reference letters for future applications. Remember, college is not only about textbooks and exams but also about creating connections and networks to support your educational and career progress.

Live Or Recorded: College Learning Options

Colleges often provide both live sessions and recorded content for learning. The choice between them hinges on individual preferences, schedules, and learning styles.

Live classes facilitate real-time interactions, enabling rich discussions, immediate clarification of doubts, and a communal learning atmosphere. They also offer a structured timetable, which can assist with time management. The main drawback is the need to match the class or professor's pace and the potential conflict with other commitments.

Conversely, the rise of recorded classes since the COVID-19 pandemic has supported the shift towards blended learning. Recorded content allows students to control their pace, pausing to take notes, replay complex sections, or fast-forward through more straightforward material. However, it does not provide the immediacy of interaction and feedback.

The optimal solution may be a hybrid approach that combines both methods to fit individual needs and time constraints. The goal is a learning method that enhances understanding and retention. Remember that active engagement with the material is essential to study effectively, regardless of the format.

Take Care Of Technology & Data

In today's digital age, safeguarding technology and data is crucial for uninterrupted learning. Well-maintained devices play a vital role in effective studying but are often overlooked.

Physical Care: Keep devices clean and well-maintained, store them in a case, and use screen protectors where necessary to extend their lifespan and performance and protect them from physical damage.

Internet Security: Exercise caution when connecting to networks, especially public Wi-Fi, to prevent data theft and maintain privacy. Install antivirus software to protect devices from malware that can compromise data. Be vigilant when downloading files or clicking links to ensure these come from legitimate and safe sources.

Keep Software Updated: Update device software regularly to ensure optimal performance and security. Updates often include patches to fix vulnerabilities.

Data Management: Regularly deleting unnecessary files and apps helps free up storage space, ensuring smooth device operation and optimizing performance.

Password Security: Use strong, unique passwords and consider a password manager to keep accounts secure, safeguarding personal information. Additionally, enabling features such as password protection can help minimize the risk of unauthorized access to sensitive data.

Privacy Settings: Take control of your information by reviewing and adjusting privacy settings on all devices and accounts.

Backup Data: Protect work by regularly backing up data to external drives or cloud services, serving as insurance for your efforts.

Mastering Time Management

Effective time management is critical to college success and lies at the heart of smart studying. It is not about the hours spent studying or pulling all-nighters but ensuring every minute counts. Organizing, prioritizing, and allocating time successfully sets the stage for better study habits and a more balanced college life.

Understanding Time Management

Time management isn't merely about tracking hours and minutes; it is about harnessing the potential of each moment to create a productive, fulfilling, and balanced college experience. As you transition from high school, you will quickly realize that the academic workload, personal responsibilities, and extracurricular activities at college demand a heightened sense of organization and prioritization.

Effective Time Management: College life is filled with academic demands, tight schedules, and vibrant campus activities. With the constraint of a 24-hour day, is it really possible to excel in studying, engage in social events, and find time for relaxation? Yes, and the answer lies in mastering time management. By effectively organizing your hours, you can enhance your academic performance, reduce stress, and ensure you have time for social activities and downtime.

Link Between Time Management & Academic Success: Have you ever observed students effortlessly balancing classes, assignments, and activities while still having time for a social life? It is not magic, but excellent time management! Allocating dedicated time slots for focused study minimizes the need for last-minute cramming. Regular review sessions boost retention and understanding, leading to better performance. Furthermore, it reduces the chance of missed deadlines or rushed assignments, ensuring high-quality work.

Time Is Precious: Recognizing and managing this effectively can be the difference between feeling overwhelmed and confidently navigating college life. Remember that the purpose of time management strategies is not to confine but to empower. Techniques are adaptable to individual requirements and can transform the entire college experience.

Self-Assessment & Goal Setting

Self-assessment requires analyzing one's strengths, weaknesses, and areas for improvement. What are you good at? Where do you tend to waste most of your time? Are you a morning person or a night owl? Knowing this makes it easier to figure out the best ways to study.

Goal setting is next. For example, what are the aims for this semester; is it to improve grades, join a club, or learn a new skill? Setting a target makes it easier to map out the route to get there and stay focused. It can then be broken down into smaller, achievable tasks with deadlines set for each one.

Identifying Personal Time Wasters: We all have them! College life is rife with distractions - from spontaneous hangouts to the call of social media. While it is essential to relax and have fun, it is crucial to identify activities that take significant time without adding value to your goals.

This requires honest self-assessment, looking at daily routines, and analyzing procrastination patterns. Recognizing these aspects allows informed decisions on adjustments and better time management.

Setting Short-Term & Long-Term Goals: Vision drives action, so it is essential to have these objectives. Short-term goals act as checkpoints and stepping stones guiding day-to-day efforts. Long-term goals are the bigger-picture objectives, like graduating with honors or securing a coveted internship. These goals provide a broader framework, guiding the overall academic trajectory.

Be "SMART!": To ensure attainable goals, they should be clear and structured, often referred to as **S**pecific, **M**easurable, **A**chievable, **R**ealistic, and **T**ime-bound ("SMART") (Doran, 1981). Goals must be revisited and readjusted periodically as progress is made, ensuring they remain relevant and on track. Setting clear and measurable goals makes study sessions more purposeful and motivates students, providing a clear path to follow.

Time Management vs Smart Studying

Understanding the relationship between time management and smart studying strategies is crucial as they work together to enhance effectiveness.

Smart studying methods boost learning efficiency and can be divided into basic and advanced. These tactics help optimize the understanding, retention, and memory of information.

Time management techniques help students allocate and organize their time to maximize productivity, reduce procrastination, and balance academic and social commitments.

Learn To Prioritize & Schedule

Not All Tasks Are Equally Important: Prioritizing means figuring out which tasks are most crucial and must be done first. Imagine: your professor has just assigned a large project, a friend suggests starting a study group for an upcoming test, and oh, there's a club meeting tonight you want to attend. Feeling overwhelmed? These clashes or demands on a student's time are common occurrences. But the key is not to try to do everything; instead, it is about focusing on the most important at the right time. Prioritization is like a personal sorting hat, guiding the decision on where to focus.

The Eisenhower Box Or Matrix - Urgent vs. Important: This tool, named after US President Eisenhower (Eisenhower, 1953; Covey, 1989), aids task prioritization and management by sorting tasks according to their urgency and importance. Imagine a box divided into four parts:

Top left: These are essential and urgent tasks - those demanding immediate attention.

Top right: For important but not urgent tasks - items to schedule for later.

Bottom left: Reserved for not essential but still urgent tasks - candidates for delegation.

Bottom right: For tasks that are neither important nor urgent – perhaps these don't need to be done.

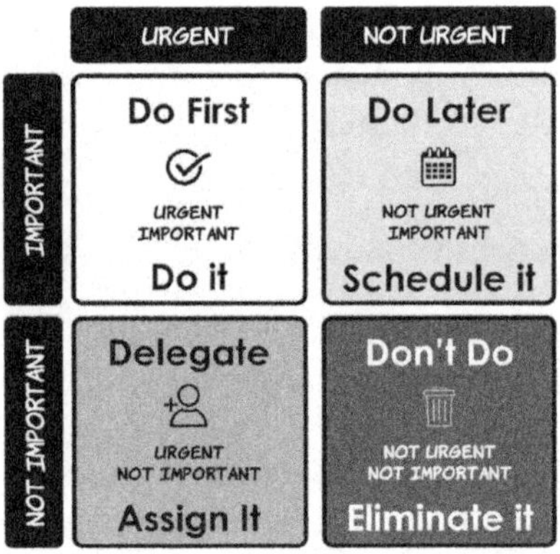

Source: https://www.eisenhower.me/eisenhower-matrix/

For example, a student could prioritize tasks using the Eisenhower Matrix:

Important and Urgent (top left): Finish and submit work due tomorrow.

Important but Not Urgent (top right): Start studying for a midterm exam which is three weeks away.

Urgent but Not Important (Bottom left): Reply to an email from a club member about a non-critical meeting happening today. Consider delegating this as it does not align with your priorities.

Not Urgent Not Important (Bottom right): Browsing social media or watching TV shows unrelated to coursework.

With so much going on at college, it may be tempting to go into a headless-chicken mode, running around trying to do it all. But there is no need to panic! Prioritization helps navigate this chaos, sorting through and focusing on the essential tasks to enhance productivity. So, when feeling overwhelmed, take charge by organizing tasks by urgency and importance.

Effective Scheduling

So, you have a ton of tasks to get done and have ranked them by priority. How can you keep track of and handle everything between assignments, club meetings, workouts, and social events? The best solution is effective scheduling. By creating a personal game plan, each task can be outlined and prioritized to achieve goals.

Create A Weekly & Monthly Study Plan: Begin with an overview. Look at the month and weeks, marking important dates such as exams and deadlines. This provides clarity of what lies ahead. Next, drill down and break these tasks into smaller chunks, allocating specific times throughout the week to tackle them. Remember, consistency is key. Regular, shorter study periods are more effective than marathon cramming sessions.

Use Digital & Traditional Planners: Digital tools and apps can send reminders and sync across devices. At the same time, traditional hard-copy planners may offer greater satisfaction in checking off completed tasks. Both methods can visually represent progress toward achieving the set goals.

Schedule Regular Breaks: Non-stop grind is not the way to go. The brain needs rest to perform at its best, so schedule short pauses during study sessions. Take a walk, grab a coffee, or listen to music to feel refreshed. It will make your study time more effective.

Master The Art of Saying "No"

College should be enjoyable and fulfilling, and balancing academics and social activities is vital to making the most of your time there. This doesn't mean saying no to fun but instead choosing experiences wisely.

This balance will be tested often, especially when tempting offers arise, such as a party or hanging out. While the appeal of seizing the moment and the fear of missing out ("FOMO") are real, having the strength to say 'No' is essential. This ensures that time is invested in meaningful and manageable activities; it is not about closing doors but intentionally choosing which ones to open.

Understand The Value of Your Time: Every hour committed to one activity is an hour taken away from another. It is all about opportunity cost. By understanding and valuing your time, you can make informed decisions about where it can be best spent.

Relevance To Set Goals: When an opportunity arises, assess whether it contributes positively or detracts from current goals. If it doesn't align, consider exercising that "No" to remain focused on your objectives.

Practice Assertiveness: Saying "No" is not dismissive or rude but the ability to set boundaries. Learn to communicate the reasons clearly and politely; greater respect is gained for those who are honest about limits.

Guilt & FOMO: Feeling regret or worry about what you may miss when declining an invitation is natural. Remember, being selective means fully engaging with the chosen opportunities rather than overextending and diluting efforts across too many fronts.

Balance Academic, Social & Personal Life

Stepping onto campus can feel like opening the door to a hectic universe with new friends, classes, clubs, and parties. But with this new freedom comes the challenge of balance.

Make Time To Socialize Without Jeopardizing Academics: The most effective way to achieve this is to plan! If a social event is coming up, either get ahead on studies or set specific catch-up times after the event. Setting dedicated times for work and social activities helps to achieve this balance.

Balance Group Projects & Personal Study: Group projects are enriching but can also be challenging, such as aligning schedules and differing work ethics. Allocating specific times for individual study is essential. Managing this requires clear communication and the use of organizational tools. Striking the right balance will maximize the benefits of group synergy and personal academic goals while cultivating teamwork, delegation, and time management skills.

Overcome Procrastination

We have all been there: the clock is ticking, and the deadline is approaching, yet we find countless ways to put off the task at hand. Procrastination can be a major enemy at college when every minute counts. However, one must first understand the reasons behind this to take control.

Identify Root Causes: Procrastination is often not caused by laziness. Emotional or psychological barriers, such as fear of failure, the overwhelming size of a task, or lack of motivation, can be the real reasons. Self-reflection, discussing with peers, or seeking counseling can help identify the underlying causes. Pinpointing these means necessary steps can then be taken to overcome any issues.

One Step At A Time! Break large tasks into smaller, more manageable, achievable segments to avoid feeling overwhelmed. This can lessen intimidation and encourage further progress. Modifying the study environment using quiet spaces, website-blocking apps, or a phone's airplane mode can minimize distractions.

Reward Yourself! Our brains inherently seek rewards, so creating tangible incentives for post-task completion can boost motivation. Whether it is a treat, a break, or a fun activity, ensure it is only awarded after finishing a task. This conditions the brain to link task completion with positive outcomes over time, reducing the urge to procrastinate.

Harness Technology

Technology is an incredible asset but can be a double-edged sword. It should be used to ensure it aids, and not distracts, the study process. With thoughtful planning, technology can be used to maximize available time.

An Aid to Learning: Apps can aid in traditional study tasks such as managing time, organizing notes, and making flashcards. Features like digital reminders can help maintain a regular study schedule and take regular breaks. Online platforms such as subject-specific websites can offer extra tutorials or lectures.

Avoid Distractions: It is essential to be aware of technology's potential to distract, such as through social media sites. Silencing notifications can help avoid the temptation to check these sites during study sessions. Also, use apps that reward focused work and switch on a device's "Do Not Disturb" feature to ensure periods of undisturbed concentration. This way, devices can be transformed from potential time wasters into powerful time management allies.

Cloud Storage: Services such as Dropbox and Google Drive help to keep documents accessible from any device and location with an internet connection. It is like carrying a personal library around with you!

Browser Extensions: These can make studying more productive by adding features to web browsers, such as blocking distracting websites, saving articles, and highlighting information.

Artificial Intelligence ("AI") & Chatbots: These can personalize the learning experience by answering questions, simplifying concepts, and identifying weak areas with recommended targeted study materials. While AI offers significant benefits, students must use it cautiously and be aware of its limitations, including the potential for inaccuracies (or "hallucinations"). It is essential to understand and verify information with sources, especially when there are uncertainties.

AI must only supplement learning rather than as a substitute to replace personal effort. Additionally, students must be aware of AI detection tools often used by academic staff when reviewing assignments, as this can have a negative impact if non-original work is identified.

Basic Essential Study Practices: Make Them A Habit!

These basic methods are like the building blocks when constructing a house. Just as a house cannot be built without a solid foundation, it is difficult to excel in studying without these fundamental habits.

Be Organized!

Being organized and planning time effectively is the cornerstone of smart studying. Use a planner to identify and track all tasks, academic and non-academic. Then, prioritize based on urgency and importance. Break down more significant projects into smaller, more manageable tasks. For instance, divide a large essay into sub-tasks such as research, outline, drafts, and final edits.

Avoid Multi-Tasking

Multitasking, like watching a movie, cooking dinner, and having a phone conversation, can compromise the quality of each. Multitasking during study sessions similarly impairs the brain's ability to process and retain information. Research suggests it can lead to more errors and less retention of knowledge (Michigan State University, 2017; USC et al., 2016; Cleveland Clinic, 2021). Thus, it is beneficial to concentrate on one task at a time.

Multitasking can be avoided by prioritizing tasks by listing and addressing them sequentially, focusing on the most critical or challenging first. This "single-tasking" approach ensures each task receives undivided attention, improving the quality of work and understanding of the material. Tools like the previously mentioned Eisenhower Matrix can aid in ranking tasks by urgency and importance.

Take Regular Breaks

Taking breaks during study sessions is essential and is not a waste of time or laziness. Research suggests it can improve focus, productivity, and creativity. Consider them as a necessary part of a study routine.

Cognitive Refreshment: Taking short pauses avoids mental exhaustion. Just like a body needs rest after exercise, regular breaks help recharge the brain, resulting in better focus and clarity.

Enhanced Retention: Memory consolidation, i.e., turning short-term information into long-lasting memories, is boosted by taking breaks. During this time, the brain absorbs and assembles the new material, leading to longer-term retention.

Prevent Burnout & Maintain Motivation: All work and no play can lead to exhaustion. Long hours at the desk can also lead to feelings of being overwhelmed, frustration, and fading interest. Stopping regularly can ease these negative emotions and maintain motivation.

The Pomodoro Technique (Crillo, 1987): This uses a timer to break work into 25-minute sessions followed by 5-minute breaks. After four cycles, a longer break of 15 to 30 minutes is recommended. This can help maintain concentration, especially for those prone to distractions, and supports a balanced, productive schedule.

Find A Conducive Study Environment

This should be a comfortable location where it is easy to concentrate and not be disturbed. For example, it could be a public library or a quiet corner in a coffee shop. A tidy, organized study spot free from distractions is crucial for productive studying. Avoid interruptions from your phone or unrelated web pages. Natural light is best, but good lighting is also essential. Some people prefer silence, while others find background noise helpful. Experiment to discover what works best for you.

Master Notetaking

Taking notes is like creating a roadmap for the learning journey. Good notes help navigate the material learned, highlighting key points to aid memory and understanding. These records are crucial, as lectures can be complex and information heavy. But it is not about scribbling down everything a professor says verbatim. It is about identifying and writing the main ideas in one's own words. This process of condensing and rephrasing helps with comprehension and retention.

There are many ways to take notes, so experiment with different methods to see which works best for you.

Liner Method: Information is written in the order in which it is presented.

Outline Method: Information is organized by main points and subpoints.

Cornell Method (Cornell University, n.d.): Notes are divided into 3 sections: information during the lecture, key points after the lecture, and a summary.

Mind Mapping Method (Buzan & Buzan, 1993): Starts with a central idea and draws branches for related points.

Remember that effective note-taking is an active process, and it is not just about copying information but about understanding it and making it your own. So, pay attention in class, take clear and concise notes, and review them regularly. This skill will help both in college and later in life.

Read Around A Topic

Reading widely and deeply entails exploring materials related to the study topic beyond the recommended core reading list. This could include additional books, articles, or videos offering varying perspectives.

Consolidates Understanding: It deepens knowledge and comprehension. Exploring a topic from multiple sources and perspectives provides a more detailed view, akin to assembling puzzle pieces to form a clearer picture.

Sparks Curiosity: It inspires interest and enhances engagement. Discovering new facts, ideas or compelling arguments from other resources can make the subject more enjoyable and encourage a proactive approach to learning rather than passively absorbing information.

Cultivate Life Skills: Reading widely when learning promotes critical thinking and openness to different ideas.

Study Groups & A Study Buddy

Studying does not always have to be alone! Participating in study groups and partnering with a friend can boost learning and make working more effective and enjoyable.

Study Groups: This is like being part of a sports team: just as each player brings a unique skill to the game, each study group member can bring a unique perspective.

Benefits: Exploring material in greater depth, learning from others, clarifying doubt, and reinforcing own understanding when explaining to others. A study group should be focused and constructive; it is not a place for gossip or distractions.

Study Buddy: This is like having an accountability partner and is a reciprocal relationship. Like having a workout partner in a gym, a study buddy can provide support, motivation, and focus.

Regular Review Over Time

Last-minute cramming may sometimes seem necessary! However, regular review and revision enhance understanding and memory, which lessens the need for intense eleventh-hour sessions. This approach reinforces knowledge and supports recall, particularly during exams. The technique of taking frequent, shorter study sessions is known as the "Spacing Effect" and has proven more effective for long-term memory retention than single, extensive study periods (APA, 2011; The Decision Lab, 2021).

Test Yourself

Enhanced Learning: Self-testing is a more effective way to boost retention and understanding than mere re-reading material. It strengthens memory by requiring active recall efforts. Effective methods include problem-solving, quizzes, flashcards, and mock exams. The more frequently one self-tests, the better the brain stores and retrieves information.

Identifies Knowledge Gaps: Testing helps pinpoint areas of weakness, as incorrect answers indicate the need to review specific topics. Self-testing can be used to replicate real exam conditions, which should help reduce anxiety and optimize performance when facing the actual test.

Integrate Self-Testing into Your Study Routine: Avoid the common procrastination of waiting until the day before the exam; instead, make self-testing part of a robust study routine. Consider doing this after finishing each module. It is a great way to maximize study effort, ultimately leading to better performance.

Incorporating basic study techniques into regular habits will boost academic performance. Just like brushing your teeth every day, these study habits must be done regularly to get the most benefit. Remember, consistent practice is key. Over time, they can make studying easier, less stressful, and more successful. They are the building blocks for good study skills and are critical to effectively studying.

Advanced Study Techniques: Taking You To The Next Level

Based on research on optimal brain learning processes, advanced study techniques take learning to the next level. These methods boost comprehension, improve long-term memory retention, and promote a deeper, more nuanced grasp of complex concepts. The suitability of these depends on personal choice and may not be appropriate for all students.

Active Learning

This involves actively participating during learning instead of passively receiving information. It is like driving a car instead of being a passenger. Driving means actively understanding the route and adhering to road rules.

Active learning encompasses various methods, such as self-explanation, teaching others, and creating your own questions and answers on the material. For example, after reading a chapter, instead of immediately moving on, take a moment to describe the content in your own words. Alternatively, pretend to teach the material to someone else.

This approach goes beyond mere reading or listening to lectures. It requires a deeper understanding of the material, leading to a more solid grasp of the topic. It involves engaging with the material, questioning it, discussing it, and applying it. While this requires more effort, it is highly effective. So, rather than being a passenger in your learning journey, take the wheel and drive!

Understand, Don't Memorize

Understanding a subject is far more important than memorizing facts because it enhances retention and the ability to apply knowledge effectively.

This is an advanced study technique because it requires a deeper level of engagement with the material. When a student grasps how to solve a math problem, for instance, this knowledge can be applied to similar problems, whereas memorization will not be as helpful due to the lack of understanding.

Grasping the material at each stage is crucial because concepts are typically developed and expanded upon in successive sessions. If coursework is not understood at every stage, it can lead to subsequent difficulties as the lack of comprehension hinders further learning. In a nutshell, one can only move on to more complex concepts if the basics have been understood.

Metacognition

Metacognition is thinking about thinking. It helps individuals manage their thinking process, plan, evaluate, and adjust their approaches to tasks, problem-solving, and learning. Students can use it to find the most effective study strategies and work more efficiently (Center for Teaching, 2018; TEAL et al. No. 4, 2019; Neuroscience News, 2021; Teachers1on1, 2021; Verywell Mind, 2021; NIH et al., 2021; UCL, 2020; LinkedIn, 2023).

One approach is to pause at intervals during studying to ask questions such as "Do I understand this?" or "Is it possible to explain this to someone else?" This practice enables the assessment of progress and comprehension while identifying areas that may require further review.

Reflecting on study strategies can also prove beneficial. Some may prefer handwritten notes, creating flashcards, or verbally explaining concepts.

Enhance Memory With Mnemonics & Memory Aids

This approach involves connecting new information with familiar concepts to create mental shortcuts for quick recall. Mnemonics come in various forms, offering practical ways to remember facts, concepts, or sequences. For instance, one common form uses phrases, sentences, or associations to facilitate easier recall of facts or concepts. For example, the phrase "My Very Excited Mother Just Served Us Noodles" helps us remember the order of the planets: Mercury, Venus, Earth, Mars, Jupiter, Saturn, Uranus, and Neptune (Mullen, 2019).

Another form is acronyms, where a word or abbreviation is created from the initial letters of a series of words or concepts. For instance, "HOMES" helps recall the names of North America's Great Lakes: Huron, Ontario, Michigan, Erie, and Superior.

In elementary education, rhymes or melodies help students memorize information, such as US Presidents or the 50 States of the USA. Visual mnemonics, like mental imagery or stories, also help students remember complex ideas.

Mnemonics and memory aids are valuable for recalling a substantial amount of information and making studying more enjoyable and effective. However, understanding the material remains the primary goal.

Interleaved Practice

Studying a single topic for an extended period can lead to monotony and reduced productivity. Interleaved practice keeps the brain engaged by alternating the subjects or types of problems within one study session. For example, in mathematics, rather than focusing on just algebra, a session could alternate between algebra, geometry, and calculus problems.

Initial difficulty is common with interleaved practice due to frequent switching; however, studies show this method leads to superior learning results. It challenges the brain to remain active when recalling information and solving problems, which enhances understanding and long-term memory retention (Neuroscience News, 2021; Teachers1on1, 2021; Verywell Mind, 2021; NIH Research Matters, 2021).

To use interleaved practice effectively, plan study sessions to include various related topics or problems, then mix it up. This helps the brain connect different ideas and hence makes studying more effective. However, balancing and spending adequate time on each topic for proper understanding before switching to the next is essential. Individuals should tailor the approach to fit their personal learning style.

It is essential to distinguish between interleaved practice and multitasking. While the former is about switching between different single learning tasks to deepen learning, multitasking involves doing several tasks at the same time, which can make it harder to focus and perform well in any single task.

Dual Coding

Dual Coding is a method that combines imagery and words to boost learning. This approach capitalizes on the brain processing visual and verbal data differently by presenting information in these two forms. It is like giving directions by describing a route while looking at a map of that journey. Some dual coding practices include:

Using colors to highlight important parts of notes.

Creating diagrams to supplement written notes.

Using color-coding to group topics or concepts.

Developing visual aids like charts or infographics.

Dual Coding can be a powerful tool for learning because it engages different parts of the brain, creating more connections to the information. Adding visuals to notes can make studying more effective as it aligns with the brain's natural way of processing information (InnerDrive Blogs, 2021; The Learning Scientists, 2016, 2019; Structural Learning, 2021; Century Tech, 2021; Simpleshow, 2018).

Effective Exam Preparation

A Structured Approach

Success in college relies significantly on a student's performance in assessments, which may include exams, midterms, finals, or substantial coursework contributions. Therefore, it is crucial to prepare effectively for these evaluations. Just as a traveler would not embark on a journey without a map, one should not approach assessments without a proper game plan. Preparing well is the key to surviving and thriving in college.

A systematic approach to exam preparation is more than mere reading and note-taking. It involves being organized, knowing what to expect, and doing your best. Being methodical reduces the chance of being caught unprepared and helps to tackle tests with confidence.

Smart study strategies, as covered earlier in this chapter, should also be used for exam preparation. These methods can be tailored specifically to enhance readiness, ensuring students can approach exams calmly and confidently when the day arrives.

Understand The Exam Format

Exams and assessments come in various forms, each requiring its own approach. It is, therefore, vital to understand these assessment types, know what to expect, and utilize resources like past papers and sample questions. There are many different types of exam formats that are dependent on the course, including:

Multiple Choice: Assesses the ability to recognize key information quickly.

Short Answer: Often requires concise responses and demands a deeper understanding of the subject.

Essay: Written submissions provide the opportunity for in-depth analysis and critical thinking.

Practical: These test the ability to apply knowledge to live situations and are common in science modules.

Oral: Involves direct discussions with the examiner. While potentially intimidating, it provides the chance to demonstrate one's depth of knowledge and communication skills.

Open-Book or Take-Home: These test the ability to synthesize information as resources such as textbooks or notes are permitted during the assessment.

What To Expect

Before walking into an exam or assessment, it is essential to know its duration, structure, and grading criteria.

Duration: The time allotted for various assessments can differ. Multiple-choice exams typically have shorter durations and require swift responses. In contrast, essay-based tests demand more time for well-thought-out, structured responses involving analysis and critical thinking. Being aware of the allotted time helps manage efforts effectively.

Structure: Assessments may consist of different sections or instructions. For example, a science exam might have multiple-choice questions, short answers, and a lab portion. Understanding this structure allows better allocation of time and effort accordingly.

Syllabus Focus & Grading Criteria: The syllabus details all the topics covered in a course, while the grading criteria outline how points are allocated for correctness, clarity, depth of analysis, and presentation quality. Understanding both enables students to prepare for exams, manage their time efficiently, and ensure their work meets the grading standards.

Past Papers & Sample Questions

As the saying goes, "Practice Makes Perfect." One invaluable resource in your preparation arsenal is past papers and sample questions. Incorporating these into your study routine certainly increases your chances of success.

Familiarity: Practicing with past exams helps make the format and types of questions more familiar. This reduces anxiety and unwelcome surprises, boosting confidence on exam day.

Content: Past papers cover questions similar to the current assessment and provide practice for structuring answers and identifying key concepts. Be aware of syllabus changes to avoid wasting time on outdated content.

Time Management: Practicing timed assessments helps allocate time effectively, develops a sense of proportion and pacing, and ensures an exam is completed within the given time.

Self-Assessment: Strengths and weaknesses can be identified by answering sample questions and comparing them with model answers. This helps focus study efforts on areas where improvements are needed most.

Create An Exam Study Schedule

A well-crafted study schedule enhances the chance of exam success. It is not only about managing time but also about covering all necessary material systematically. This can make the difference between cramming all night and confidently walking into the exam room prepared and composed.

Start Early: Preparing well in advance provides several advantages:

Less Stress: Avoids last-minute cramming, thereby reducing anxiety associated with eleventh-hour panic study sessions.

Greater Retention: the Spacing Effect (i.e. reviewing material over time) enhances long-term recall.

Understanding, Not Just Memorizing: This is more likely, as early preparation allows time to fully grasp concepts and course material .

Break Exam Topics Into Parts: Separating study material into smaller portions makes planning a study schedule more manageable.

Topic Breakdown: Divide the course material into distinct topics or units. This provides clarity about what needs to be covered.

Allocate Time: Determine how much time to allow for each topic. Be realistic by considering the difficulty and familiarity with the material.

Tackle The Most Challenging Topics First: Not all subjects are created equal, and some are more difficult than others. Unless prerequisite knowledge of other subjects is needed, prioritizing these more difficult areas allows more time to seek clarity and provides a positive mental boost upon completion. This approach also ensures that time is allocated where it matters most.

Identify & Prioritize Key Topics: Recognize which areas are particularly important for the exam. These might be provided in the course syllabus, by the academic staff, or in the grading criteria.

Set SMART Goals & Milestones: Goal setting is a powerful motivator and aids in focusing and staying on track. Set targets for each portion; for example, aim to complete a certain number of chapters by the end of the day. Also, consider sharing these goals with a study partner to increase accountability.

Allocate Specific Times To Study: This is essential for creating a structured routine. Choose consistent times that align with your natural rhythms. Some students may be more alert in the morning, while others may be night owls. Also, respect your study schedule! Treat study sessions as seriously as a class or a job. Avoid distractions during these dedicated study hours.

Include Regular Breaks: A study schedule must incorporate regular breaks to optimize learning. Use the previously mentioned Pomodoro Technique, for example, taking pauses from studying to stretch or move around, doing something different to re-energize the brain.

Make The Most of Resources & Materials

Having the right resources and materials when preparing for exams is akin to being equipped with the tools necessary for a successful mission.

Textbooks, Lecture Notes & Supplementary Materials: These are the primary sources of information; read them thoroughly because they provide comprehensive coverage of the course material.

Lecture notes also provide valuable insights and additional information not found in textbooks. They offer the lecturer's perspective and can help clarify concepts discussed in class.

Professors may recommend additional materials like handouts and study guides. Using these resources alongside textbooks and notes deepens understanding and shows a commitment to mastering the subject.

Online Resources & Databases: The Internet is a treasure trove of information, including academic platforms, videos, and databases, that can assist with exam preparation. Social media platforms such as Facebook enable students to engage with others and gain insights. However, choosing credible sources relevant to the field of study is essential.

Library & Academic Support Services: The college library can be a goldmine of resources that should not be forgotten. Librarians can assist in finding relevant books, articles, and research papers. Additionally, many libraries offer quiet study spaces conducive to focused learning.

Academic support services such as tutoring centers offer valuable assistance. Tutors can give additional clarity while writing labs can help hone essay-writing skills, an invaluable asset for exams involving essay questions.

Review Sessions, Extra Classes & Use Your Professors! Many professors offer review sessions or extra classes leading up to exams. These sessions are tailored to help students consolidate their knowledge, ask questions, and clarify doubts. Attending them can provide invaluable last-minute insights and reinforce the understanding of critical concepts.

Another often overlooked resource is your professors. Don't hesitate to seek their assistance during office hours or at the next class. It is a great way to receive specific, even one-on-one support and demonstrates dedication to your subject and studies.

Healthy Lifestyle & Stress Management

Preparing for exams can often lead to feelings of stress and anxiety, and time pressures can mean staying healthy takes a backseat. It is essential to stay healthy and manage stress. Later chapters will cover in-depth information on how to maintain health for a balanced life at college. Below are the key areas specifically relevant to exam preparation.

Get Enough Sleep: Sleep and rest are pivotal in memory retention and learning.

Eat a Balanced Diet: Include brain-boosting foods and maintain proper hydration to ensure optimal brain function.

Exercise Regularly: This boosts cognitive function and acts as a natural stress reliever; it helps to maintain clarity and focus.

Moderate Caffeine Intake: Avoid the temptation of excessive caffeine or other stimulants during study sessions. Overconsumption can lead to jitteriness, disrupted sleep, and compromised focus.

Try to Relax: Techniques such as meditation or deep breathing exercises can ease the feeling of being overwhelmed and help bring a sense of calm.

Positive Affirmations: Cultivating a positive mindset can reframe challenges and boost confidence.

Seek Support: Talking with peers, tutors, or counselors can be an outlet for airing concerns and helps to maintain clarity and perspective.

The Day Before

What you do the day before an exam can significantly impact performance and reduce unnecessary stress on the actual exam day.

Review, Don't Cram! If you have prepared well in advance, then cramming at the eleventh hour will not be necessary. Instead, simply skim over the main points to refresh memory and reinforce understanding. This also prevents feeling overwhelmed, which cramming often brings.

Be Organized: Ensure all necessary items are gathered, such as stationery, IDs, calculators, etc. Confirm the exam location and starting time. Review transportation (if the exam is not online) and have backup travel options in case of any issues.

Online Exams: Ensure a stable internet connection and all necessary tech components are working and charged. If possible, secure a quiet space and inform others to avoid disturbances during the exam.

Relax & Unwind: Allocate some time for relaxation in the evening and resist the urge to study late into the night. Light reading, meditation, or calming activities can help alleviate nerves.

Get a Good Night's Sleep: Ensuring quality sleep is crucial to maintaining a fresh and relaxed mindset on the exam day. While knowing course content is essential, one's state of mind is equally important.

On The Day

The day of the exam represents the culmination of all the hard work and preparation, so make the most of it! Here are some essential tips on how to approach exam day with confidence:

Have A Healthy Breakfast: Begin the day with a nutritious breakfast to optimize brain function. Foods rich in complex carbohydrates, such as whole grains, and protein sources like eggs or yogurt can provide sustained energy. Avoid sugary cereals and excessive caffeine, which may lead to energy crashes or jitteriness later.

Arrive Early & Avoid Rushing: Punctuality is crucial, and rushing can cause you to feel flustered and anxious. Arrive early at the test location to allow time to settle in and review any last-minute notes. For online assessments, test technology and connections ahead of time. Consider placing a "Do Not Disturb – Exam in Progress" sign on the desk (if in a public space) or door to minimize the chance of being disturbed.

Pre-Exam Relaxation: Take a few minutes to relax and envision success – this can improve overall mental performance. Breathing deeply, meditation or visualization can help calm nerves and enhance focus.

Read Questions Thoroughly: When the exam starts, resist the urge to dive right into the questions. Instead, start by carefully reading all instructions. Pay attention to specific guidelines on format, time limits, and question types. Misinterpreting these can cost valuable points.

Answer The Question! While obvious, answering the question asked is crucial. Students often make the mistake of providing a brain dump of everything known about a subject as soon as they see certain trigger words in a question. To avoid losing marks, it is critical to thoroughly read and understand what is being asked, ensuring that an appropriate and specific answer is provided.

Remember the earlier discussion on grading criteria and mark scheme? No matter how great the information is, marks may not be given if the question is unanswered or falls outside the assessment guidelines.

Exam Time Management: This is key to tackling all the questions within the allotted time. After reading the instructions, quickly scan the entire exam to understand its structure and point distribution. Allocate time for each section or question based on its difficulty and point value, but don't be afraid to adjust if necessary. Working through old test papers under timed conditions when preparing for exams will ensure familiarity.

Review Answers: If you're all done before time is up, resist the temptation to finish and hand papers in immediately. Exams are not tests of speed but accuracy - **<u>always</u>** use any remaining time to review answers. Look for errors, missing information, or overlooked questions. Even a quick check can catch mistakes, allowing valuable corrections to be made.

Post-Exam: Learn from Your Experience!

After resting and recovering from the intensity of exams, analyzing the experience is vital, as it helps to prepare for future assessments.

Reflect On Performance For Better Preparation Next Time: This review is an essential post-exam routine. Consider what went well and what didn't. Was time managed effectively? Were there problem areas? This review allows insights into strengths and areas that require improvement. Apply the lessons learned from one exam to future preparations.

Don't Be Too Hard On Yourself: While identifying errors is essential, it is also important not to beat yourself up about it. Remember that everyone makes mistakes so try not to dwell on them. Instead, analyze what could have been done better with a positive and constructive mindset. Determine why mistakes were made and how they can be avoided next time. View mistakes as stepping stones and great learning opportunities.

Reward Yourself: The exam preparation process can be mentally and emotionally demanding. After the event, treat yourself to a well-deserved reward. It could be as simple as enjoying a favorite meal, watching a movie, or spending time with friends. These actions are positive mental boosts that acknowledge dedication and provide a well-earned mental break before studying restarts.

Being able to study smartly can make an enormous difference to your college life. The building blocks of a robust study routine start with practical and basic study techniques, like managing time effectively, knowing how to set goals, and learning to prioritize. These techniques are like the roots of a tree, giving a firm foundation on which to build.

After the basics, more advanced techniques can be used, like active learning, metacognition, and understanding instead of memorizing. These are like a tree's branches, helping you reach higher and learn more effectively. Techniques like Dual Coding, mnemonics, interleaved practice, and leveraging technology can also boost learning.

Finally, exams and assessments culminate the learning journey, and thorough preparation is the key to exam success.

Remember, the goal is not just to study harder but smarter. Understanding and using these methods maximizes the available study time and achieves a balance in college life. Your commitment to mastering these techniques will be the key to boosting your academic potential and achieving your goals. So, start planting your study tree today, and watch your learning grow!

Chapter 5

Friendship Dynamics: Challenges & Strengthening Bonds

" Strangers are just friends waiting to happen."

Rod McKuen

Starting college is a thrilling time, as you have the chance to meet people from different backgrounds and perspectives. This diversity can enrich your experience, providing a broader understanding of other viewpoints and enabling personal growth. Yet, the transition can also be stressful, as building new friendships can present its own set of challenges. Many experience homesickness, anxiety about making new friends, or conflicts with roommates. Remember, you are not alone in this; others feel the same and are just as eager to connect and form friendships.

In this section, we address common concerns that newcomers often face, building upon the discussions in Chapter 3 on meeting new people during Orientation Week. There will also be insights and practical tips on handling these common worries and thriving socially with confidence and resilience.

As a new student, you may receive a deluge of advice from those who have been in your shoes. While this guidance is well-intentioned, your journey in building friendships is unique. Although helpful, others' advice and experiences should not be seen as a strict blueprint. The challenges you encounter may differ, but take comfort in knowing you are not alone. Embrace advice that resonates with you, but keep in mind that the path to college friendships is yours alone to explore and learn from.

While every student's college experience is personal, please be reassured that any concerns are not unique, and generations of students have experienced the same and survived!

Overcoming Shyness & Finding Your Footing

Meeting an entirely new group of people can be daunting, especially for those naturally shy or introverted. Feeling anxious about introducing or conversing with strangers is normal; remember, it is okay to feel this, and others will feel the same.

Take Small Steps: There is no need to immediately dive into large social events or be uncomfortable. Start by initiating simple, low-pressure interactions. This could be as simple as saying hello to someone in your dorm or asking a classmate about a homework assignment. Over time, these small exchanges gradually build up confidence in approaching new people.

Take Advantage Of Groups: Leverage situations where interactions are more natural. Join clubs or engage with groups that match your interests. Participating in group activities provides a natural way to start conversations and make meeting people less intimidating.

Be Patient: Making new friends takes time; it is about progress, not perfection. Being more settled in a new environment will make meeting new people easier and more natural.

Starting Conversations

Initiating a chat with strangers or new acquaintances can be daunting. Common worries include finding what to say, keeping a conversation going, and fear of embarrassing yourself.

It's Not Just About Talking: A good conversation involves speaking and listening. Show interest in the other person by asking about their opinions or interests. This takes the pressure off you and makes the other person feel valued and more likely to talk. Also, remember to share your interests and experiences to establish a connection.

Not Every Silence Is Awkward: It is natural for conversations to have lulls. Instead of panicking, use these moments to collect one's thoughts or steer the conversation in a new direction. It is also okay to acknowledge not knowing what to say; honesty can often lead to more meaningful conversations.

Suggested Icebreakers: Consider trying some of the suggestions listed in Chapter 3.

Practice Is Key: Don't give up but keep going! Remember, every good conversationalist was once a beginner. With time and practice, starting and maintaining conversations will become easier.

Feeling Overwhelmed

College life often has exciting yet potentially overwhelming social events and numerous unfamiliar faces. Whether it's dorm meet-and-greets, club recruitment events, or introductory classes, the rapid pace and volume of social interactions can sometimes feel too much.

There is no need to rush or feel frantic; take it all slowly and proceed at your own pace. Choose events that match your interests and prioritize quality interactions over quantity. If large gatherings feel daunting, seek out smaller gatherings or one-on-one opportunities.

Additionally, set aside some quiet moments for yourself, such as leisurely walking or listening to music. Allocating time for relaxation and recharging is essential. As time passes and everyone settles in, the pace of social events will naturally become more manageable.

Fear Of Rejection & Being Judged

Trying to meet new people or make new friends can sometimes trigger fears of rejection or judgment. It is natural to want to make a good impression and fit in.

Many Share These Fears Too: College is also new for other first-years, and most want to be accepted and liked. The fear of rejection or judgment is a universal human experience. Try to view others with empathy, understanding that they may be dealing with similar concerns.

Self-Worth: It is natural to seek validation from others, but the most crucial approval comes from within. So, believe in yourself, value your unique qualities, and let the opinions of others carry less weight. Embrace who you are and find confidence in your individuality.

Be Resilient: Accept that not every social interaction will go perfectly. Rejection and criticism are parts of life, whether at college or post-graduation. Don't take these moments too personally or let them define your identity. Instead, learn from these experiences and treat them as opportunities for growth rather than setbacks. However, seek support from close friends, family, or college counseling services if you are struggling. Trust yourself and know that these fears will become less daunting with time.

Peer Pressure & Finding Your Tribe

College can sometimes pressure one to fit in or change oneself to be accepted. It is natural to want to belong; however, steer through this in a healthy and authentic way.

College Is A Place Of Diversity, Not Uniformity: It brings students from varied backgrounds and cultures together, so it is okay to be different! Rather than feeling pressured to fit a specific mold, embrace your individuality and appreciate the diverse nature of your peers.

Make The Right Friends: Changing superficial aspects of oneself to fit in may seem like a quick solution, but it often leads to feelings of dissatisfaction in the long run. Feeling the need to adjust indicates that the social circle may not be fully compatible; avoiding falling into the wrong group of friends is essential. A solution is to expand the social circle to meet others with similar interests or sense of humor. Explore more clubs, activities, and social events. The broader the social circle, the greater the chances of connecting with people naturally.

Genuine connections and authentic friendships are built on shared values and sincerity. There is no need to befriend every person encountered. Instead, concentrate on discovering those with whom a real connection is felt and nurture those relationships.

Cliques & Social Groups: On campuses, it is normal to see social groups already in place, which can be intimidating for newcomers who might feel like outsiders. Remember, though, that the formation of these groups around shared interests is a natural occurrence. These groups often serve as excellent opportunities to find potential new friends.

Many of these social groups are dynamic and open to new members who share their interests. Therefore, don't be discouraged from approaching them. Just be sure that any chosen groups align with your interests and values.

Handling Peer Pressure: There may be situations where individuals feel compelled to do something that doesn't align with their values just to fit in with their peers. In such cases, it is crucial to uphold personal boundaries. Saying no is perfectly fine. People who genuinely value a friendship will respect individual choices and opinions. Ultimately, college is about personal growth as much as academics. Staying true to one's values will lead to finding real friends.

Coping With Feelings Of Loneliness

Entering a new college environment can sometimes trigger feelings of loneliness or exclusion. Recognizing that these emotions are normal and can be overcome with time, patience, and adequate support is essential.

Temporary Emotions: Starting college marks a significant transition, and it is natural to experience periods of loneliness or feelings of isolation. However, these moments are fleeting and will not define your college experience. It is worth noting that many other students may also be grappling with similar feelings, even if they do not show it. So, exercise patience as these emotions will pass.

Reach Out To Others: Actively seeking opportunities to connect, such as joining study groups or attending social events, can help counteract feelings of isolation. Reaching out to roommates or classmates can provide relief; they may relate to your feelings or offer a fresh perspective. Maintaining contact with old friends and family can also provide comfort amid the new environment.

Do Something Enjoyable: This could be reading a book, exercising, or listening to music. Positive activities can distract from negative emotions and create opportunities to connect with like-minded people. While it is healthy to have some time alone, it is time to seek companionship if it starts feeling like isolation.

Seek Professional Assistance If Necessary: If persistent negative emotions affect your mental well-being or academic performance, it may be time to seek help from a trained professional. Many colleges have counseling centers that provide resources and support for managing these feelings.

Dealing With Conflicts Or Misunderstandings

In college, just as in life, conflicts and challenging individuals are inevitable. Disagreements are a natural part of any relationship and do not necessarily mean the end of a friendship. Handling conflicts maturely can strengthen the bond and deepen mutual understanding and respect. Remember, you do not have to get along with everybody, and it is perfectly acceptable to have differences; what truly matters is how these situations are managed.

Open Communication: Maintain composure and approach the person involved to discuss the issue clearly and respectfully. Do not hesitate to address the problem promptly; the sooner it is resolved, the better for everyone involved. Avoid making assumptions, jumping to conclusions, or becoming overly emotional.

Don't Forget To Listen: While getting your point across is important, listening to and considering the other party's viewpoint is equally vital. Always provide them with an opportunity to explain their side.

Show Empathy: Try to be patient and understand the situation from the other person's perspective. Acknowledging their viewpoint can diffuse a situation and lead to a more productive conversation.

Seek Help When Necessary: If the situation escalates and a resolution cannot be reached independently, consider involving a neutral third party, such as college staff or a counselor. They can mediate the discussion and ensure it remains respectful and productive.

Dealing With Bullies

Facing bullying can be a challenging and distressing experience, but it is crucial to remember that nobody should endure intimidation. Everyone should feel safe and respected in their environment.

Recognize Bullying: Identifying this behavior is essential; it can range from name-calling, physical harm, or threats to subtler actions like exclusion, spreading rumors, or persistent negative comments.

Assert Yourself: Maintain confidence and calmly inform the bully that their actions or words are unacceptable. Always prioritize safety; walking away and seeking help is better than engaging in a confrontation if the situation escalates.

Stay Calm & Resilient: Try not to engage or retaliate in such situations, as this can often worsen the situation. Bullies often thrive on getting a reaction, so showing composure and not being intimidated can sometimes discourage them from continuing.

Persistent Bullying: If this behavior continues, document all instances, noting dates, times, locations, and potential witnesses. This evidence can be valuable if the matter needs to be escalated. Reporting the person may be necessary to ensure it stops and protects others from similar behavior.

Don't Suffer In Silence: Reach out to trusted friends, family, or counselors, as their support can provide vital strength. Taking care of one's emotional well-being is crucial, and there is no shame in seeking assistance when needed.

Report Bullying: Colleges have policies and resources to address bullying, including counseling services, resident advisors, and campus security. Reporting the incident to the appropriate authorities enables them to act and help.

Facing bullies can be tough, but remember, seeking support is never a sign of weakness. Embrace the journey, and remember, you can overcome any obstacle!

Building Meaningful Connections

Steering through the college social landscape can seem daunting, especially for new students. Making friends is essential to the college experience, but it isn't always easy. It requires a combination of openness, effective communication, and a willingness to engage in various social activities.

However, it is essential to remember that every individual's journey is unique. Making friends can be quick for some, while others may take longer to form meaningful connections. The goal should not be to make a specific number of friends but to build meaningful relationships.

Get Involved

College offers a variety of activities beyond regular classes. Clubs, sports teams, study groups, volunteer opportunities, campus events – you name it! These are excellent platforms for meeting people with similar interests, making initiating conversations and forming connections easier. For instance, a student who enjoys soccer could join the college soccer team or a soccer fan club and meet others with the same interests. A student who loves music could find a band or choir to become involved in.

Shared activities, such as attending guest lectures or joining study groups, can broaden your social network and create opportunities for meaningful conversations and memorable experiences. This can help strengthen bonds with others who have similar interests and goals. Working towards a common objective or sharing exciting moments creates a sense of camaraderie and community that can solidify new friendships. Stepping out of your comfort zone by exploring new activities can lead to discovering new passions and lasting friendships.

Remember that friendships can also thrive on diversity. Connections formed with people of different interests can challenge and enrich your perspectives as well as introduce new ideas. The key is to be respectful and understanding when building meaningful relationships.

Be Open & Approachable

Making friends starts with being willing to meet new people and showing a genuine interest in others by listening to them. Being approachable plays a crucial role in forming new connections. Consider this: a person is generally more inclined to talk to someone with a friendly smile than someone who is frowning and seems closed off. Therefore, try to be conscious of your body language. Keeping eye contact during a conversation, showing genuine interest, and providing appropriate reactions can make you appear friendly and approachable. So, keep an open mind, wear a friendly smile, and go ahead and meet some awesome new friends!

Take The Initiative

There is no need to wait for people to come to you. Being the one to start a conversation or suggest an activity is a brilliant way to make new connections. Although it may sometimes feel daunting, taking the first step shows you are friendly, and people often appreciate someone taking an interest in them.

Start A Conversation: Good conversation starters can be simple questions, like asking about their day or thoughts on a recent lecture. Sharing a little about yourself can make the other person more comfortable and open up.

Organize Something: Taking the initiative is about creating opportunities to connect. If a club meeting or event is on campus, why not invite someone from your class or dorm? You could also arrange a study group for a class you are all taking. These shared experiences can help to break the ice and create a foundation for friendship.

Don't Be Discouraged: Sometimes, people may respond differently than hoped but don't be put off. Not every conversation will lead to a strong friendship, and that's perfectly normal. The key is to keep trying.

Be Sincere

Be Genuine: Authenticity is necessary to build lasting friendships, and students must stay true to their values. College marks a fresh beginning, and the temptation to change or conform to fit in or impress others can be strong. However, the strongest friendships are built on honesty and authenticity. Staying true to one's interests, values, and beliefs is crucial, and increases the chance of cultivating real and long-lasting friendships.

Be Kind & Respectful: These are universal qualities that everyone appreciates. Treating others the same way you would like to be treated is fundamental. Friendship involves a reciprocal exchange, and being mindful of others' feelings and ideas is essential.

So, remember to be yourself; sincerity is attractive. Embracing one's uniqueness and staying genuine will attract friends who appreciate and respect the real you, resulting in more fulfilling and enduring friendships.

Respect Diversity

College is a fantastic place to meet people from different cultures, backgrounds, and walks of life. Understanding and appreciating this diversity can be an enriching educational experience.

It involves engaging with diverse groups to broaden one's understanding of the world. It is more than tolerating differences - it is about embracing them with respect, empathy, and curiosity. It not only helps personal growth, but also teaches interpersonal skills vital in the post-college world.

Quality Over Quantity

While having a large social circle is great, remember that meaningful friendships are about quality, not quantity. A handful of close friends who offer understanding and support can prove far more rewarding than numerous casual acquaintances.

Authentic friendship goes beyond mere socializing; it is built on trust, mutual respect, understanding, and being there for one another. If friendships don't form immediately, don't stress. Genuine connections take time to develop, often evolving gradually over shared experiences and requiring effort from both parties. Patience is vital, so allow quality friendships to develop naturally over time.

Remember, this is not a popularity contest! Instead of trying to be friends with everyone, focus on nurturing friendships that provide comfort, value, and happiness. These friendships will enrich your college life and may even last a lifetime.

Effective Communication

Communication is essential in any relationship, be it friendships or otherwise. It is about more than just talking; it includes listening, understanding, showing empathy, and responding appropriately. The ability to communicate well will facilitate making connections and building friendships.

Learn To Listen! Listening is crucial as it shows the thoughts and opinions of others are valued. It encourages open dialogue and mutual understanding. So, when someone is speaking, give them your full attention. Avoid distractions and resist the urge to interrupt or rush the conversation.

Express Opinions Clearly: When sharing ideas, ensure they are clear and easily understood. Be open and honest, and respect other people's feelings and perspectives.

Non-Verbal: Communication that does not involve words is also essential. This includes eye contact, body language, physical gestures, and facial expressions, as these can also convey interest, empathy, and understanding.

Disagree Respectfully: It is natural sometimes to have different opinions or disagreements. What is essential is being able to appreciate alternative viewpoints and address issues in a respectful and understanding manner. It is possible to disagree without being disagreeable.

Reciprocity

Friendships are built on respect, support and understanding. It should also be a two-way street and not one-sided. Reciprocity means a mutual give-and-take where both parties must put in the effort and contribute to the relationship. This doesn't mean keeping a score but ensuring both parties feel valued, supported, and heard. Over time, as the friendship deepens, greater familiarity means this balance often naturally develops. Maintaining a balance between give-and-take ensures no one feels taken advantage of and supports a more positive and fulfilling relationship.

Reciprocity also means respecting each other's time, boundaries, and interests. If a friend dedicates time to an event you love, it is vital to reciprocate by participating in something they enjoy. Similarly, if they have been a supportive listener, be ready to lend an ear when they need to vent.

Be Patient

Starting college often brings a desire to make friends promptly due to the new environment and the need for a sense of belonging. However, it's crucial to recognize that forming meaningful friendships is a gradual process that develops over time through shared experiences, trust, and understanding. Patience is vital; avoid rushing or forcing connections.

People adapt to new environments at their own pace, so it's important to avoid comparing yourself to others. Don't be discouraged if it takes longer to find a social circle.

Being patient also means giving people a chance, as first impressions may not accurately represent someone. Consider giving them another opportunity to connect unless initial interactions are negative or toxic.

Getting to know people takes time; there's no need to feel pressured to make a specific number of friends within a set timeframe. Cultivating a few genuine relationships over time is more valuable than hurriedly forming many superficial ones. So, take your time, practice patience, and authentic friendships will naturally develop.

Starting college is a time marked by the excitement of meeting new people and the challenge of adapting to new surroundings. Having friends is essential as they offer support, help alleviate stress, and together create unforgettable memories. They can also be fantastic study partners and expand your social circle. While making friends can vary from person to person, it's essential to do this at your own pace, only joining activities or study groups that align with your goals and interests.

Remember, the quality of these relationships is more important than the quantity. Be patient, as it takes time for genuine friendships to deepen naturally through shared experiences. These connections not only enhance your college life but also have the potential to become lasting bonds that continue long after graduation.

CHAPTER 6

SURVIVING ROOMMATES: LIVING IN PEACE & HARMONY

" Peace is not the absence of conflict, it is the ability to handle conflict by peaceful means."

Ronald Reagan

It's All About Communication & Compromise

Having a roommate is often an integral part of the college experience, and while it can be rewarding, it certainly presents its own set of challenges. Remember that this is a temporary and not a permanent situation. In time, you and your roommate will move on to different phases in your lives.

A harmonious living space thrives on collaboration. Creating a supportive environment that encourages work, rest, and social interaction supports a sense of community and warmth. Respect and compromise are also essential tools for peaceful living. It is vital to realize that this is a two-way street: if you expect your roommate to consider your needs, you must also be open and willing to listen to and work with them. Appreciating and applying these principles will make shared living an enjoyable and fulfilling experience.

Open & Honest Communication

Clear communication is the foundation of a healthy roommate relationship. It involves expressing your thoughts, concerns, and expectations respectfully and openly, allowing your roommate to share their input and perspective. This helps prevent confusion and misunderstandings and ensures all roommates agree regarding cohabitation rules and habits.

Set Expectations Early

This is a crucial first step after moving into the dorm. Discuss what each person expects from the other, such as cleanliness standards, noise levels, study hours, sleep schedules, and shared item usage. For instance, one person might be an early bird who prefers to study in the quiet of the morning, while the other might be a night owl who does their best work late at night. Establishing these expectations upfront can help manage expectations and accommodate each other's routines.

Note that setting expectations should not be a one-time event but a regular process of negotiation and adjustment. As the semester progresses, new commitments mean updating your roommate on developments and revising agreements as necessary. Adaptability and respect for each other will contribute to a harmonious shared living experience.

Listen & Be Considerate!

Listening means giving full attention when your roommate is talking to show respect for their feelings and concerns. Put away distractions like phones and laptops and make eye contact. Listening allows you to pick up non-verbal cues, like body language and tone of voice. This creates a supportive and friendly atmosphere in your shared living space.

Listening also helps with conflict resolution. Hearing your roommate's perspective makes finding compromises and solving issues easier. It reduces misunderstandings, builds trust, and can make time together more enjoyable.

Consideration is also crucial in any relationship. Respect each other's needs, habits, and personal space, as your actions affect each other. Be mindful of how activities like playing music, having guests, cleanliness, and sleep schedules might impact your roommate.

Being considerate also means understanding your roommate's feelings and perspective. You are different people, and how you view or treat something does not mean that the other person would handle it in the same way. So, check in if they seem upset or uncomfortable and give them space if they have had a rough day. If they upset you, communicate directly instead of being passive-aggressive. Keep in mind that it is their living space as well; therefore, treat each other with kindness, respect, and understanding, just as you would wish to be treated.

Privacy

Even though it is a shared living environment, everyone still needs time and privacy. This includes physical space, like not going through your roommate's belongings without permission, and personal time, where they might need some quiet hours to study, relax, or be alone.

Privacy is not just about solitude but also about respecting personal information. This means understanding that some topics might be off-limits unless your roommate chooses to share them. Furthermore, if your roommate does confide in you, it is essential to respect their trust and keep their information confidential unless permission has been given to share it. Navigating privacy can be tricky, especially in the close quarters of a dorm room. Still, talking matters through and mutual respect can help both parties feel comfortable and secure in the shared living space.

Compromise & Choose Your Battles!

It is normal to encounter differing opinions, habits, and preferences, and being able to compromise is vital to maintaining harmony. For instance, one roommate may prefer a cooler room, but the other wants a warmer environment.

Compromise requires open-mindedness, empathy, and flexibility from both parties. It is about listening to your roommate's perspective and expressing your own. It might involve negotiation and, sometimes, sacrifice. A compromise ensures that both parties feel heard, respected, and comfortable in their shared space. Remember, it is not about "winning" or "losing" but about finding a solution that caters to both parties' needs. This process resolves potential conflicts and encourages a stronger, more understanding relationship.

Remember, living with someone else always requires a certain degree of compromise. Sometimes, letting minor annoyances slide might be better than picking a fight over every little matter.

Setting Expectations: Typical Issues

Having an early conversation about mutual expectations is crucial. This ensures both parties are on the same page and understand each other's needs. Approach these discussions with respect, an open mind, and a willingness to compromise. The goal is to prevent misunderstandings and coexist harmoniously.

Sleeping Patterns: Night Owl Or Early Bird?

Sleep patterns may seem minor, but they can significantly impact how well roommates get along. For instance, if one person is wide awake when the other is trying to sleep, it can lead to friction. Do you tend to stay up late working, or are you an early-to-bed, early-to-rise person? Knowing each other's typical sleep schedule will help you find workarounds to avoid disturbing each other and ensure both get adequate rest.

It is not only about sleeping and wake-up times but also about night and morning routines. Perhaps one person likes to read with a bright light before sleeping, while the other prefers complete darkness. Or one may need their alarm to go off at full volume, while the other prefers a gentler wake-up. Discussing these matters upfront allows the opportunity to come to an agreement.

Studying Habits

Discussing study habits is crucial as it can significantly impact academic success, so it is essential to understand each other's needs.

Consider preferences for late-night versus morning study sessions, or complete silence or background noise while studying. Collaborating to establish mutually preferred study times and locations is essential to avoid disrupting each other's studies.

Additionally, consider the shared space. If it is a small dorm room, there might not be separate areas to retreat to during study time. Negotiating specific quiet hours for the room or agreeing to use headphones during working periods is vital. Exploring alternative study spots outside the room, such as libraries or common areas, is another option worth discussing.

Visitor Policy

Roommates must have clear guidelines regarding visitors, including friends, significant others, or visiting family members. Maintaining a balance between personal privacy and accommodating social interactions is essential for harmonious living. Be sure to communicate openly and promptly address any concerns or plan changes. Be proactive where possible, as this is more effective than addressing issues after they arise.

Establishing a well-defined visitor policy can prevent misunderstandings and manage expectations. Consider including the following details:

Who is allowed to visit?

Designated visiting hours.

Limits on the length of stays.

Overnight guest policies.

Maximum number of visitors at any given time.

Whether guests can be in the room without that roommate's presence.

Advance notice requirements for upcoming visits.

Informing your roommate of impending visitors is courteous. It allows them to plan their activities accordingly, such as studying in a different location, to ensure more space and privacy during the visit.

Even with a guest policy, flexibility is essential, as this allows for adjustments or last-minute plans. Or perhaps adopt an open-minded approach to accommodate spontaneous gatherings or unexpected visits.

Balancing Noise, Silence & Individual Needs

Maintaining a balance between noise and quiet in shared accommodation is crucial, necessitating conversations on issues such as music volume, TV usage, and specific quiet hours. Discussing these preferences can cultivate mutual respect and promote harmony between roommates. For example, keeping the room quieter the night before an 8 a.m. class or during late-night study sessions is considerate. To accommodate these needs, use headphones or limit the number of visitors during quiet hours. Also, many individuals value personal downtime and moments of solitude. The goal is to create a relaxed, undisturbed environment that respects everyone's space.

Cleanliness & Shared Responsibilities

One of the most common issues is cleanliness and household responsibilities. While the definition of "clean" can vary from person to person, being upfront about preferences and establishing clear standards can help manage expectations and avoid misunderstandings.

Solutions to provide clarity could be to establish a rotating task schedule or agree on each person's responsibilities. Clearly defining roles ensures the workload is distributed fairly through structured weekly cleaning days or a flexible understanding of personal clean-up requirements. The goal is to prevent tension from one person feeling they are shouldering all or most of these responsibilities.

Note that shared obligations go beyond just cleanliness and can encompass expenses for common supplies, such as shared grocery lists or replacing used items.

Health, Cultural & Religious Considerations

Students must be aware of and respectful of others' medical and cultural backgrounds.

Health & Allergies: To create a safe living environment, take the time to learn about any medical conditions your roommate may have and inform them about your health issues, if any. This could include severe allergies, specific medications, or any health-related needs. It may involve setting aside separate food storage areas, using certain products carefully, or recognizing when someone requires downtime due to health reasons.

Culture & Religion: College often brings students from diverse cultural and religious backgrounds together. These differences can influence daily routines, dietary choices, celebrations, or moments of prayer and reflection. Therefore, being open and accepting of cultural or religious practices is essential. For example, if one roommate observes a religious day of rest or follows specific dietary guidelines, understanding these practices can prevent misunderstandings or disruptions. The key is to embrace and respect diversity, viewing these conversations as opportunities for learning and personal growth.

Safety & Security

Ensuring the safety of the shared space is crucial. Addressing these concerns and respecting each other's boundaries creates a trustworthy and secure environment for both.

Physical Security: This involves ensuring that windows are secure, locking the door at night and when everyone is out, and deciding who holds a spare key. Feeling safe is essential for peace of mind and avoiding unexpected or uncomfortable situations.

Personal Possessions: The security of personal belongings in a shared living space must be considered. Having designated areas for personal belongings and lockable storage for highly valuable or sensitive items can be helpful.

Digital Security & Etiquette: These include using shared devices, not sharing passwords, and respecting each other's privacy when using technology. In today's digital age, ensuring online safety and privacy is as important as locking the front door.

Recognizing & Respecting Personal Boundaries

Living with roommates often means blending different worlds into one shared space. Acknowledging and respecting personal boundaries and privacy within this space is essential. Upfront discussions about these matters help prevent misunderstandings or overstepping the line.

Shared vs. Personal Items: It is crucial to differentiate between communal items, like a sofa or kitchen utensils, and personal belongings, such as journals, laptops, or certain foods. To avoid future conflicts, discussing which items are off-limits and which can be shared when you first move in is advisable.

Personal Boundaries: This concerns an individual's emotional and personal space. Not every moment is suitable for sharing, and students often require some solitude or quiet time for reflection. Perceptions of these boundaries can vary between individuals, so establishing them early on is essential. This may involve agreeing to knock before entering, refraining from prying into personal matters unless invited or recognizing cues that indicate the need for time alone.

Once established, respecting boundaries is equally important. Even if they may seem insignificant to you, they matter to your roommate. Unintentionally violating them can lead to tension and conflicts. If this happens, it is essential to apologize, discuss the issue, and reaffirm the expectations for the future.

Conflict Resolution

Disagreements are a natural part of any relationship, but how they are handled can make the difference between a tense or a harmonious living situation.

Deal with Issues Promptly: Letting problems fester can build resentment and create a tense environment. Address concerns as they arise to prevent them from escalating into major conflicts.

Stay Calm & Respectful: How a problem is handled can affect its outcome. A composed and thoughtful approach will more likely result in a receptive roommate. An emotional outburst, however, could risk alienating them.

Communicate Clearly: To prevent misunderstandings, express concerns precisely, directly, and respectfully.

Listen & Be Receptive: Ask roommates for their thoughts and listen to their concerns. This validates that their opinions matter and demonstrates your willingness to understand their viewpoint.

Negotiate & Compromise: Approach disagreements with a problem-solving mindset to find solutions that satisfy both parties' needs. Be willing to compromise and choose your battles wisely.

It's Not About Winning: The goal is not to assign blame or win arguments but to find workable solutions for both parties.

Apologize & Forgive: Offer a sincere apology when you are wrong and forgive when your roommate acknowledges their mistake. This clears the air and helps restore a happier environment.

Move Forward Positively: Learn from past issues, revise expectations, and find ways to minimize future conflicts. Maintain a positive relationship by spending quality time together and strengthening your bond.

How To Express Your Feelings

It is essential to have an open and honest conversation with your roommates respectfully without making the situation worse. Clearly expressing your concerns without assigning blame is necessary. Choosing a calm time to convey your feelings is best to avoid putting your roommate on the defensive.

Be aware of passive-aggressive language, as it can often worsen the situation. Avoid "You" type statements; instead, use the word "I" as it is less antagonistic. For example, "I feel stressed when there is a lot of noise while I'm studying - can we agree on quiet hours?" is far less aggressive than saying, "You stress me out when you make so much noise when I'm trying to study." Below are some tips on phrasing concerns less aggressively for different potential situations.

For Noise:

"You" statement: "You always play your music so loudly. It's really annoying."

"I" statement: "I find it hard to concentrate when the music is loud. Could we maybe use headphones during study hours?"

For Cleanliness:

"You" statement: "You never clean up after yourself in the kitchen!"

"I" statement: "I feel overwhelmed when the kitchen is cluttered. Could we discuss a cleaning schedule?"

For Guests:

"You" statement: "You always have your friends over, and it's really intrusive."

"I" statement: "I sometimes would like quiet time to relax or study. Could we discuss how we can set times for guests coming over?"

For Shared Items:

"You" statement: "You keep using my stuff without asking!"

"I" statement: "I'm uncomfortable when my belongings are used without my knowledge. Can we set some boundaries about sharing items?"

For Personal Space:

"You" statement: "You're always in my space, and it's really invasive."

"I" statement: "I value my personal space and time. Could we discuss ideas about respecting each other's space please?"

Tough Roommate Situations

One of the most significant adjustments for many students is sharing a living space with someone whose lifestyle, background, or values differ significantly from their own. Below, we will address common challenging situations and provide practical advice for handling them.

The Selfish Roommate

A selfish roommate acts primarily in their own interest, often neglecting their fellow occupants' needs, feelings, or comforts. Their inconsiderate behavior could include consistently leaving shared spaces messy, unauthorized use of your belongings or food, excessive noise during your study or sleep times, or failure to contribute to shared responsibilities.

Starting a conversation with a roommate about their behavior can be difficult. Thus, choosing an appropriate time when both parties are in a good mood and have a positive attitude is essential. Start by initiating an open conversation about the issues, being specific about what bothers you without directly blaming them. For instance, instead of saying, "You always leave the kitchen messy," say, "I feel upset when I find the kitchen messy." This approach may lead to positive changes if your roommate is unaware of the impact of their actions.

Additionally, clear boundaries and shared responsibility guidelines should be established. These rules can cover chores, sharing food and other items, and setting quiet hours for study and sleep. Clearly defined expectations make it easier to hold each other accountable.

The Grumpy Roommate

A grumpy roommate often displays crankiness or a bad temper. Their irritability can be sporadic or part of their general character. Managing this can be challenging, as their moodiness can create a stressful living environment.

Don't Take It Personally: Remember that your roommate's irritability may not be about you, and they could be dealing with personal issues or stress.

Show Your Concern: Consider initiating a gentle conversation with them. Choose a time when they seem less grumpy, and gently express your observations and concerns about their mood. For example, "I've noticed you seem upset a lot, and I'm worried about you." This approach shows that you care and can help prevent them from becoming defensive.

Maintain A Positive Environment: Keep shared spaces clean, occasionally make shared meals, or suggest doing something you enjoy together. This can help boost the overall mood and lessen their irritability.

Time To Get Specific: If their mood still does not improve or they are venting their frustrations on you, it is necessary to address the issue. Tell them the impact of their behavior on you and encourage them to seek help if they are struggling with stress or other problems. Remember that caring still requires setting boundaries and not taking on the role of therapist.

Look After Yourself: If their negative attitude does not improve and begins to affect your well-being, distance yourself from them and perhaps spend more time outside the dorm room. If necessary, seek advice from a counselor or a trusted advisor.

The Nasty Roommate

A nasty roommate often displays unkindness, rudeness, or even malicious behavior through their actions or words. They may consistently disrespect your personal space, engage in insults or belittlement, exhibit aggression, or create uncomfortable situations. Hygiene may also be an issue, leading to dirty or unsanitary shared spaces. This hostile living environment can significantly affect your well-being.

Address The Situation: Tell them assertively that such behavior is unacceptable. Avoid engaging in retaliatory "tit-for-tat," which could escalate the situation. Remember, you have the right to feel safe and respected.

Maintain Firmness & Composure: When dealing with a nasty individual, communicate reasonably and respectfully. Choose a relaxed, distraction-free moment to express your feelings without making accusations. Highlighting how their behavior affects you can help reduce defensiveness and promote a constructive conversation.

Establish Clear Expectations: Discuss, among other things, standards for respect, privacy, and shared responsibilities. Remember that both parties must agree to and respect these boundaries for them to be effective.

Document Incidents: Consider keeping a confidential record of specific incidents, including dates, locations, descriptions, and any evidence of the behavior. Ensure your roommate is unaware of this, as it could exacerbate the situation. Such records can be valuable if you must involve college authorities or seek legal assistance.

Seek Help: While it is important to initially try to resolve the situation, if the behavior continues and becomes threatening or abusive, do not hesitate to seek help from college authorities. Safety must always come first. Discuss your situation with a trusted friend or advisor, and then contact campus security or even local law enforcement if the abusive behavior continues.

The Thieving Or Dishonest Roommate

This roommate tends to take items that do not belong to them or regularly tells lies. They might borrow items without permission or even steal them outright. This deceitful behavior can extend to lying about various matters, from who is responsible for messes in the shared space to more significant issues like unpaid bills or missing or broken items. Dealing with such a roommate can cause unease and mistrust, making your living situation uncomfortable.

Address The Issue Promptly: Lying or stealing is a serious matter that requires immediate attention. For minor theft (like eating your food without asking), address it directly in a non-confrontational way. For example, you could say, "I've noticed some of my things have gone missing recently. Do you know anything about this?" Remember to express concerns without making direct accusations. Your roommate may not fully realize the impact of their actions, and bringing it to their attention might be sufficient to rectify the situation.

If The Behavior Persists: It is time to reiterate or establish clear boundaries. To remove temptation, store valuables in a secure, inaccessible place for your roommate. Discuss expectations regarding privacy and respect for personal belongings. Request that they ask first before borrowing anything and do the same yourself to ensure mutual respect.

Severe Cases: Consider involving housing staff or campus security for more serious situations, such as major thefts or repeated dishonesty about significant issues. This goes beyond typical roommate disagreements. Document incidents and keep any evidence, such as photos of missing items or text messages, to support your case. Always prioritize safety and well-being in such situations.

The Intoxicated Roommate

This refers to a roommate who frequently consumes alcohol or drugs excessively to the point of impairment rather than occasional use. Their behavior may be characterized by excessive noise, disruption, unpredictability, or an inability to care for themselves or the shared space. Dealing with a stoned or wasted roommate can be challenging, as their actions may not be rational and could lead to uncomfortable or unsafe situations.

Prioritize Your Safety First: Someone who is intoxicated is likely to be desensitized and unable to think or behave rationally. Be aware of this and remove yourself from the situation if their behavior becomes dangerous or threatening. Contact local law enforcement or campus security if necessary. While showing care for your roommate is important, avoid constantly looking after them or cleaning up their mess if their behavior doesn't change.

Talk to Them When Sober: Have a calm and honest conversation about their repeated behavior when they are sober. Express concerns about their health, inquire about the reasons for their actions, and discuss how their behavior affects your living situation. Use non-confrontational language to reduce the likelihood of escalation.

Seek Help For Addictions: If you suspect that their behavior is due to dependence on alcohol or substances, suggest seeking outside help. Many colleges offer free, confidential counseling services or can provide resources for local addiction support groups. Encouraging your roommate to seek help demonstrates that you care about their well-being.

Prioritize Your Well-Being: Protracted exposure to an intoxicated roommate can negatively affect your physical and mental well-being. Seek support from friends, family, or campus resources if needed.

The Roommate's Partner: Three's A Crowd

When a roommate's significant other becomes an unofficial third resident without an agreement, it can intrude on your comfort and privacy. Their presence or behavior, such as overt displays of affection, loud disputes, or inappropriate conduct, disrupts the shared living environment and must be addressed. It's important to remember that only the roommates, not their partners, have rights in the shared space.

Initiate Dialogue: The first step is to have a respectful conversation. Roommates must understand that individuals have different expectations about guests and might need to realize the inconvenience caused.

Agree To Boundaries: Proposing fair guidelines ensures both roommates' needs are considered. The importance of ongoing communication is vital to preventing future conflicts.

Define Visit Terms: Agreeing on the frequency and length of the partner's visit helps to keep the living arrangement comfortable for everyone.

Shared Space Use: To ensure equal access and privacy for all roommates, discussing guidelines for using common areas when a partner is present is necessary.

Be Flexible: Both parties should be open to adjusting the guidelines as situations and preferences change.

Guideline Specifics: Designated visiting hours and limits on the duration of stays should be set. These terms should be flexible depending on the situation. Behavioral guidelines could include moderating public affection, taking arguments outside, and respecting shared spaces and privacy.

The Promiscuous Roommate

Living with someone frequently bringing different romantic partners back can create discomfort and disruption in a shared living environment. When addressing this situation, it is crucial to talk openly about your feelings and concerns regarding their behavior.

Consider initiating a conversation about revisiting or setting boundaries regarding overnight guests. This discussion should cover aspects such as when overnight guests are permitted, the frequency of stays, and the necessity of providing advance notice before arrival.

Furthermore, it emphasizes the importance of respecting shared spaces and each other's comfort within the living environment. This includes being discreet and considerate, and intimate activities should be conducted to respect the privacy and comfort of all roommates.

If your roommate disregards your concerns or the behavior persists, mediation through your resident advisor or the housing office may be necessary. These resources facilitate constructive dialogue and find mutually agreeable solutions to such issues.

What To Do If The Problem Remains?

Seek Help!

If issues remain unresolved, seeking additional help and resources to address these challenges may be necessary.

Prioritize Well-Being: The living environment can significantly impact a student's overall college experience and academic success. It is vital to take the required steps to address any continuing roommate problems, however difficult the decisions may be.

Contact the Resident Advisor or Housing Coordinator: They are typically trained to handle disputes and provide further guidance or mediation. They can offer valuable support and assistance in resolving roommate conflicts.

Utilize College Counseling Services: They can also help students facing challenging situations. Consider seeking assistance in managing any stress or emotional discomfort arising from the ongoing issues with your roommate.

Document Incidents: Record each relevant incident, including dates, times, and details. This evidence may be needed if further escalation or legal assistance is required.

Consult College Authorities: When feeling constantly unsafe or having one's rights violated, it may be time to escalate the matter to campus authorities. This could include contacting the Dean of Students or Campus Security for further assistance. Colleges usually have policies to protect student's rights to a safe and comfortable living and studying environment.

Consider A Room Change

If the situation fails to improve or begins to negatively impact your mental health or academic performance, consider alternative accommodation and request a room change. While it may feel unfair that you are considering moving out instead of your roommate, prioritizing your mental and emotional well-being is paramount.

Make this decision after careful deliberation and only when all other attempts to resolve the issues have been tried. Several circumstances might warrant this decision, including:

Persistent disregard for agreed-upon rules.

Invasive behaviors.

Actions that consistently cause significant stress.

Regular disruptions that affect studying or sleeping.

A shared environment that feels unsafe.

Also, consider logistical factors and potential consequences when contemplating a room change, such as adjusting to new roommates and moving. While relocating to new accommodation may seem like the solution to current roommate issues, it is essential to weigh the possibility of encountering new challenges.

Do not let concerns about inconvenience or judgment from others dissuade you from taking this step if you believe it is necessary. Your college years should be characterized by personal growth, meaningful learning, and fulfilling experiences. If a room change is needed to facilitate this, then it is a decision worth making.

The transition to college life introduces a range of new experiences and obstacles, with sharing a living space often posing as one of the most significant challenges for students. Addressing potential issues early on can establish a foundation of mutual understanding and respect between roommates. Open communication is at the heart of a positive roommate relationship. While there will be inevitable hiccups, a willingness to discuss and compromise is essential. Both parties must feel listened to, valued, and at ease.

However, even with the best-laid plans, not all roommate pairings will be perfect. Dealing with a challenging roommate is a reality for many students. Knowing when to compromise, when to stand firm, and when to seek external assistance or mediation is vital. Also, realize that every individual is dealing with their own challenges, so exercising patience is essential.

Ultimately, the roommate experience, whether harmonious or challenging, offers valuable lessons in life. It teaches the importance of compromise, empathy, and effective communication - skills that extend well beyond the confines of the dormitory.

CHAPTER 7

NAVIGATING ROMANTIC RELATIONSHIPS

" A healthy relationship will never require you to sacrifice your friends, your dreams, or your dignity."

Dinkar Kalotra

Beginning a romantic relationship in college can be an exciting experience. However, it is also important to balance personal life, academics, and social commitments. This chapter provides practical guidance on general scenarios and experiences to help you make informed decisions. However, it is essential to remember that every relationship is unique, with its dynamics and challenges. Therefore, this guide should be a general starting point rather than a definitive rulebook.

While it is normal to have ups and downs in one's love life, if you experience difficult situations or feel significant stress, seeking help from friends or trained advisors is always advisable. College is a time of learning, exploration, growth, and often romantic relationships. Navigate these relationships with care, respect, and understanding, and prioritize your well-being.

The Change From High School To College

Transitioning from high school to college marks a significant change that affects many areas of life, particularly personal relationships. During this time, students often rethink their social and romantic needs, leading to personal growth and a better grasp of what they value in relationships.

The social scene in college can be quite different from the high school experience. A wider social network and the chance to forge new connections can bring excitement mixed with uncertainty and apprehension.

The independence and autonomy of college life allow students to make their own choices about dating and time management. While this freedom is liberating, making thoughtful decisions consistent with long-term objectives and core values is vital.

It is also important to appreciate that not everyone needs or wants to be in a romantic relationship during college. If you are in this category, do not succumb to peer pressure or settle for unsuitable partners.

Fundamentals For A Healthy Partnership

A healthy relationship is when both individuals feel loved, valued, and respected. This means caring for one another, listening to feelings and opinions, and treating each other with kindness. Being genuine is essential. Both parties should feel comfortable being themselves without fear of judgment or criticism. It is like being part of a team, with both parties working together to improve the relationship. Remember that a healthy relationship should bring security, joy, and positivity to your life.

Communication Is Key

Communication is the link that connects two people in a relationship. When thoughts, feelings, and experiences are discussed, this mutual sharing leads to a deeper understanding of each other, building trust and respect. Like talking to friends about what is happening in your life, doing the same with your partner is vital.

However, communication is not only about talking; listening is equally essential. Paying attention and showing genuine interest is necessary when your partner speaks, as it demonstrates respect. While disagreements are common, hearing each other's perspectives can help resolve differences in a healthy way.

Note that communication is not always verbal. People often express their feelings through actions, facial expressions, or body language. For example, if your partner seems unusually quiet, they may be experiencing difficulties. It is crucial to recognize these non-verbal cues and inquire about them.

Trust, Honesty & Forgiveness

Trust and honesty are two critical pillars of a successful relationship. You must have faith in your partner and trust they will not deceive or betray you. Honest communication strengthens this trust, allowing both partners to express their feelings and resolve conflicts constructively. Consistency in actions and transparency about intentions further cement this foundation. In return, it is equally important for you to be honest, keep promises, and remain faithful.

Forgiveness is also essential for maintaining trust and honesty in a relationship. It involves releasing bitterness and acknowledging that everyone makes mistakes. True forgiveness means learning from such moments and moving forward together rather than dwelling on the past. While it does not excuse harmful behavior, it distinguishes between intent and error, allowing trust to be rebuilt through empathy and mutual respect.

Respect & Equality

Respecting your partner means recognizing their worth and affirming their equal standing in the relationship. This respect means valuing their opinions, considering their feelings, and treating them with the kindness you seek for yourself. Disrespect, through belittlement or any form of emotional or physical harm, is unacceptable.

Equality ensures that both individuals have the same influence, sharing control and decision-making. From household chores to choosing dinner spots, decisions should be made together. While taking turns is okay, it is unacceptable if one person consistently dictates all choices. A balanced approach, with neither partner dominating, is essential for a fair and healthy partnership.

Healthy Boundaries

Relationships thrive on mutual respect and understanding, with boundaries an essential component. It is crucial to set healthy boundaries, whether relating to physical intimacy, time spent together, personal space, or anything else that matters to either person. It is also essential to openly discuss and understand each other's limits. Awareness of and acceptance of boundaries prevents misunderstandings and enhances security and comfort within the relationship. Remember, your partner is not a mind reader, so it is essential to talk to them!

Acknowledging and honoring boundaries also means accepting that 'no' means 'no.' When one party expresses discomfort, it is imperative to respect their stance without pressure. It is also essential to be able to communicate your discomfort or reservations, even if it may disappoint your partner. A partner who genuinely cares will respect your boundaries and wishes.

Managing Long-Distance Relationships

Maintaining a relationship when one partner attends a different college can be challenging, particularly when there are limited opportunities to visit each other. Feelings of loneliness, sadness, or insecurity can arise due to the absence of regular contact and curiosity about a partner's new friends or fun experiences.

Staying in touch can also prove challenging due to differing schedules and new college obligations. The lack of face-to-face interaction or regular conversations may increase the chance of misunderstandings.

There are ways to maintain long-distance relationships successfully, but it requires patience, understanding, and commitment from both parties.

Talk Regularly: Establish clear guidelines to ensure both partners feel satisfied and connected. This includes agreeing on the frequency and method of communication, such as phone calls, video chats, or texts.

Be Honest & Transparent: Discuss feelings, concerns, and experiences openly with your partner. Transparency fosters honesty and strengthens the relationship.

Establish Trust: Trust is fundamental in any relationship. Allow your partner the freedom to enjoy their college experience while maintaining boundaries and fidelity.

Manage Jealousy: Address any feelings of jealousy or insecurity constructively with your partner. Openness and communication are crucial to overcoming these challenges.

Encourage, Don't Hinder: Avoid restricting your partner or limiting your college experience due to fear of how it may impact the relationship. Be supportive, flexible, and stay in regular contact. Remember, love can thrive alongside personal growth and independence.

Support Each Other's Goals: Encourage and support each other's academic, personal, and career ambitions. Knowing that you have each other's backs can help alleviate some of the challenges of being apart.

Arrange Visits: Plan visits to spend time together whenever possible; these strengthen the sense of unity and provide the excitement of future reunions.

Stay Upbeat: Focus on the positives of the relationship and college experience rather than dwelling on the challenges that distance can create.

Relationship Types: Hookups, Casual & Serious

There are varied relationship types in college. Some students have serious relationships, dedicating themselves to a partner and considering the future together. Others prefer something more casual, enjoying company and fun without commitment. And then there are hookups, centered mainly on physical attraction and often without an emotional bond.

Casual relationships and hookups offer an exciting and carefree way to meet new people and enjoy new experiences. It is vital to communicate intentions clearly so that everyone involved understands and agrees. Misrepresenting one's desires is unfair; for example, pretending to seek something casual when the objective is something more serious.

Serious relationships, in contrast, involve more commitment and often a deeper emotional connection. They can also provide greater support and companionship. However, they also require more work, such as communication, understanding, and a willingness to compromise.

The type of relationship chosen, be it serious, casual, or just a hookup, is entirely your decision. To avoid future emotional complications, always be open about your preferences and intentions, respect the other person's feelings and boundaries, and make decisions that reflect your own values.

First Dates: Do's & Don'ts

It is natural to feel a mix of excitement and nervousness when going on a first date. Here are some pointers to ensure a successful outing:

Do's:

Be Yourself: Dress appropriately for the occasion; choose comfortable clothes that boost confidence and reflect your personality.

Be Calm: Nerves are common, so try to stay relaxed and behave naturally.

Listen Actively: Show genuine interest in your date's stories and opinions and respond thoughtfully.

Ask Questions: Prepare a few conversation topics to keep the discussion flowing smoothly.

Show Respect & Courtesy: Throughout the date, demonstrate kindness and consideration.

Have Fun: Be positive, enjoy the experience, and get to know each other.

Say Thank-You: Follow up afterward with a thank-you message or call.

Don'ts:

Arrive Late: Punctuality shows reliability and respect for your date's time.

Talk All The Time: Ensure both you and your date have the chance to contribute and share thoughts.

Discuss Controversial Or Sensitive Topics: Avoid areas such as politics or past relationships that could create tension or discomfort.

Drink Too Much Alcohol: It is essential to stay clear-headed and in control of your actions.

Make Assumptions: It is easy to judge someone based on superficial factors. Keep an open mind and give your date the chance to reveal their true self.

Spend Excessive Time On Your Phone: This behavior is disrespectful and suggests a lack of interest, which can make your date feel undervalued.

Feel Pressured To Move To The Next Stage: Do not feel obligated to escalate the date to a more romantic or serious level. Moving at a comfortable pace that feels right for you is perfectly acceptable.

Remember that it is okay if the first date does not go perfectly and that only some dates will lead to a second one. The primary goal is to learn more about each other and enjoy the experience. So, relax, be yourself, and embrace the opportunity to connect with someone new.

Online Dating & Apps

Online dating and apps have become very popular and convenient ways to meet new people, especially if you are busy with classes and other responsibilities. However, it is vital to be careful. Always protect personal information and remember that people online may not always be who they say they are. When meeting someone in person, choose a public place and tell a friend where you are going.

Just like in-person dating, online dating should be done respectfully and honestly. While many may use these platforms to meet and get to know like-minded people, some are only interested in having casual hookups. Always be clear about your intentions and respect the other person's feelings and boundaries. And if someone makes you feel uncomfortable, it is okay to disconnect and report them if necessary. While dating apps make meeting people easier, using them responsibly and safely is vital.

Dating Safety

Safety must always be a top priority. Whether meeting someone new or going on a few dates, it is crucial to inform a trusted person of your whereabouts and expected return time. Opt for public meeting places until you feel comfortable with your date, and trust your instincts; if something feels off, remove yourself from the situation.

Protecting personal information is crucial, especially when engaging through dating apps or online platforms. Refrain from sharing sensitive details like home addresses or school schedules until trust is established. Should any individual cause discomfort or behave inappropriately, utilize the safety features on apps, such as blocking or reporting.

Remember, staying safe also includes sexual safety. Ensure always that any sexual activity is consensual, and use protection to prevent STIs and unwanted pregnancies. Remember, you can decline if you feel uncomfortable. Your body, your choice. Always.

Balancing Studying & Romance

Romantic relationships can be a fulfilling part of college life, but these must not detract from educational goals. Balancing your studies and personal life can be challenging yet manageable with careful planning.

Education must always be the priority - after all, the main aim of going to college is to prepare for the future. This does not mean avoiding dating but rather ensuring that any romantic relationships support academic efforts rather than hinder them. Setting dedicated study hours and allocating times for your partner can help manage both commitments.

Communication is vital. Sharing study goals and the efforts required to achieve them can help your partner understand your needs, particularly during times of high stress or heavy workload.

It is also okay to occasionally shift focus. There may be times when academics require more attention and other times when your relationship needs nurturing. The key is finding a healthy equilibrium, ensuring your education is not compromised.

Handling Difficult Situations

Breakups & Rejections

Experiencing breakups or rejections can be challenging, especially when the ex remains ever-present on campus, in the same social circle, or is in a new relationship. It can feel like a punch in the gut, evoking sadness, anger, or even loss. However, it is essential to recognize that these emotions are normal and part of the growth process. It is necessary to work through these feelings and understand that healing takes time.

Self-Care Is Essential: During this emotional time, prioritize activities that bring happiness and tranquility. These could be spending time with friends, watching a favorite movie, or exercising. Focusing on positive activities can provide comfort and relief.

Maintain Your Routine: Keep to your daily routine and schedule as much as possible. This consistency can help establish a sense of normality and structure amidst the emotional upheaval.

It's Good To Talk: Don't hesitate to reach out for support - there is no need to suffer alone. Whether it is a friend, family member, or college counselor, talking to someone can provide comfort, guidance, and a fresh perspective.

Patience Is Key: Although it may be tough initially, time is a great healer. Try to see this as a learning experience with a better understanding of what will be required in the next relationship. Navigating this period also builds resilience for any challenging times ahead. As the dust settles, you may recognize and accept that this relationship was not meant to be. Embracing these lessons will strengthen and better prepare you for future relationships. Remember that an ending or rejection does not mean you are unworthy of love. Everyone deserves love, and the right person will come along in time.

Infidelity

Infidelity, or cheating, occurs when one partner breaches trust in a romantic relationship by engaging in intimate or sexual interactions with someone else. Experiencing infidelity can be incredibly painful, whether during college or later in life. When trust is shattered, it often leads to feelings of hurt, confusion, and anger. If faced with this situation, the first step is to remain composed to avoid irrational reactions.

Stay Calm: It is natural to feel upset or enraged, and it may take time to process these emotions. Seeking support from trusted individuals, such as friends, family, or a counselor, can provide comfort and guidance.

Talk With Your Partner: When ready and if feasible, try to talk with your partner about why it happened. It can be a tough conversation, but it is necessary for understanding and healing. This also allows you to ask questions and evaluate whether the relationship is worth salvaging. If your partner refuses to talk about it, this may answer the question of whether the relationship has a future.

Your Partner's Choice, Not Yours: When infidelity occurs, it is crucial to recognize that your partner's actions do not define your worth or value. Cheating is a choice made by the other person, and you should not shoulder the blame for their decisions despite common occurrences of victim-blaming. It is common to experience feelings of self-doubt or low self-esteem following infidelity. Remember, you are not responsible for your partner's decision to be unfaithful!

Maintain Self-Respect: Honesty, loyalty, and respect within a relationship are paramount. A partner should value and respect the boundaries of a relationship. If these are violated, standing up for yourself and letting your partner know this behavior is unacceptable is imperative.

Time To End It: Knowing when to end a relationship is crucial, especially if faced with disrespect. It is essential to prioritize personal well-being and uphold one's dignity. Be courageous, and remember that your feelings and self-respect matter.

Toxic Relationships

Toxic relationships are often marked by manipulation, control, emotional abuse, and disrespect. Consistent feelings of being drained or devalued signal this toxicity. Healthy relationships, in contrast, thrive on support, understanding, and mutual respect. Frequent feelings of unease, anxiety, or negative self-perception linked to a partner's actions may indicate a toxic partnership. Key warning signs include constant criticism, manipulation, boundary violations, and any form of abuse.

The first step to resolving this situation is recognizing and acknowledging it exists. This can be hard and may take time, especially if you have a strong emotional bond with your partner or tend to blame yourself. Share your feelings with trusted friends, family, or a counselor. They can offer advice and assistance as you work through this challenging situation.

Addressing a toxic situation may mean having discussions with your partner about their behavior, seeking professional help, or even ending the relationship. Prioritizing your emotional and mental well-being is vital, even if it means making difficult decisions. Remember, being alone is preferable to being consistently brought down in a relationship. Everyone deserves respect, love, and happiness. Do not settle for anything less.

Peer Pressure

Peer pressure is the influence of friends that may lead individuals to engage in certain behaviors or make specific decisions. However, it is essential to distinguish between sincere advice and peer pressure. While suggestions from friends often stem from genuine concern and support, peer pressure is about feeling the need to conform to their expectations or desires, even when it is not necessarily in your interests.

For relationships, this pressure may compel the individual into situations such as starting or ending relationships, engaging in sex or certain types of sexual activity, or behaving in specific ways towards their partners.

When facing this situation, remember that everyone's experience is unique. Just because a friend is dating or acting a certain way in a relationship does not mean you need to do the same. Individuals should feel empowered to move at their own pace and make choices that align with their values rather than conform to others' expectations.

Resisting this pressure and standing up to friends can be difficult but necessary to maintain self-respect and integrity. Talk to them about your discomfort with their comments about your relationships. True friends will understand and support you. Remember, your relationships, your rules.

Rushed Relationships

Meeting new people when starting college is exciting, and some may appear to be quickly jumping into relationships. While it may be tempting to follow suit, doing this hastily without taking the time to get to know the other person can lead to unhappiness or conflict. It is important to establish mutual respect and understanding before committing to a partnership.

The primary problem with rushed relationships lies in the absence of genuine connections. These require time to develop from shared experiences, trust, and understanding. Skipping these crucial steps may leave individuals feeling unfulfilled and disconnected, leading to misunderstandings.

There is no need to pursue a relationship in haste; taking a slower pace is acceptable. College is a time for academic, social, and personal exploration. Allow friendships to develop naturally, take the time to understand your relationship preferences, and let romantic connections evolve at their own pace. Remember, relationships should enhance your college experience, not add stress and detract from it. So, proceed at your own pace, and know there is no rush to commit to anyone.

Romantic & Sexual Pressure

It is essential to understand that everyone has the right to make choices about their body and the nature of their relationships. No one should feel compelled to engage in any activity that does not feel right. Saying no is completely acceptable, regardless of previous agreements, others' opinions, or any set expectations. Personal comfort and safety should always come first.

If experiencing pressure, try to address the issue with the person involved. If that is not feasible, seek support from a trusted friend, family member, or counselor who can advise and help manage the situation.

Leaving an uncomfortable situation is always an option; a respectful and safe relationship is non-negotiable. A partner who disregards your decisions or boundaries may not be the right match for you. In such instances, putting yourself first and taking actions that serve your best interest is critical.

Importance of Consent & Safe Sex

Why Consent Matters

Consent is fundamental to any romantic relationship, signifying an active agreement to engage in intimate activities. It must always be explicit, informed, and mutual, with the understanding that it can be withdrawn at any time. Disregarding or violating consent is a serious offense and can lead to harmful situations, including sexual assault. College campuses provide policies and resources to educate about consent and support victims of sexual assault. It is essential to be fully informed about these resources and to understand the true meaning of consent.

Definition Of Consent: Consent is when all parties involved in an activity agree to participate willingly. It must always be clear, ongoing, and capable of being revoked at any moment.

Consent Applies To All Aspects Of A Relationship: Consent is not limited to only sex but extends to all aspects of a relationship, including sharing personal information and physical contact like holding hands or hugging.

Always Verify Consent: Consistently seek and respect your partner's boundaries. If there is any uncertainty or hesitation, pause and communicate openly. Ensuring that your partner is comfortable with the activity or situation is paramount.

Consent Is Ongoing: It should be a continuous process, not a one-time event. Just because consent was given once does not mean it applies forever. Situations and feelings can change, and what was once agreed upon might not be okay in a different context or time.

Impact Of Alcohol & Drugs: Individuals under the influence may not be capable of providing valid consent. In such cases, it is best to wait until both parties are sober and capable of making clear, informed decisions.

Respect Fosters Healthy Relationships: Understanding and honoring consent are integral to healthier and more fulfilling relationships. Respecting each person's autonomy and boundaries is fundamental to any thriving relationship.

Safe Sex & Contraception

Understand The Risks: Practicing safe sex and using contraception is crucial for students, regardless of relationship status. This involves taking responsibility for preventing unwanted pregnancies and sexually transmitted infections (STIs) by using protection, such as condoms, for every sexual activity. Condoms are the most common method to protect against STIs and pregnancy, but they must be used correctly and checked for expiration dates.

Prevent Pregnancies & STIs: Contraception focuses on preventing pregnancies and includes methods like birth control pills, intrauterine devices (IUDs), injections, patches, condoms, and more. Each method has benefits and potential side effects; what works best will vary from person to person. Discussing the best option for you with a healthcare provider is essential. However, most forms of contraception do not protect against STIs, so using condoms in addition to another method is recommended.

Both Must Be Responsible: Both partners should share the responsibility of practicing safe sex, and one should never assume that the other will take charge of this unless already explicitly agreed upon. It is essential to have open conversations about contraception and STI protection before becoming sexually active. This applies to all types of relationships, whether long-term, casual, or with a new partner. Remember, it is okay to refuse sex if you or your partner are not ready or unwilling to use protection. Protecting your health and wellbeing is paramount. Remember - your body, your choice.

Independence & Self-Worth

In a healthy romantic relationship, self-worth and independence are essential. It is important to recognize that a relationship is a choice, not a need, and one's value is not dependent on being part of a couple.

Independence: While relying on your partner for support is acceptable, it is also essential to be self-sufficient and preserve aspects of your life that are distinctively yours. This could include hobbies, friendships, or personal goals independent of your partner. Achieving a balance between sharing your life with someone and retaining independence is vital for a healthy relationship.

Self-Worth: A strong sense of self-esteem and self-reliance helps make better partner choices. You are less inclined to settle for unsuitable partners when you value yourself.

Resilience: A solid self-worth foundation can be beneficial when handling breakups or rejections. It provides the resilience necessary to bounce back from setbacks and view such experiences as opportunities for personal growth rather than mere losses.

Developing self-worth and maintaining independence can lead to healthier relationships, which can contribute to overall happiness and fulfillment during college and beyond.

College is a time for students to mature and form meaningful connections. Romantic relationships, with their complexities, are often part of this experience. Such relationships should be built on communication, trust, and respect, with setting boundaries being essential for mutual understanding. While online dating apps offer a convenient way to meet people, it's essential to approach them with caution and awareness, especially regarding safety. Prioritizing physical and emotional health is crucial, particularly when practicing safe sex and maintaining individuality. Balancing academic pursuits with romantic and social life can be challenging but teaches valuable lessons in prioritization and time management.

When one's love life does not pan out as expected, heartbreak may follow. Although the pain may feel all-consuming at the time, rest assured that it is transient and will pass. What does last, however, are the lessons learned, the resilience cultivated, and the self-discovery that empowers you to navigate future relationships and life's challenges with wisdom.

Remember that the insights provided are intended as a general guide, as each romantic relationship and its circumstances are unique. Every experience, whether good or bad, contributes to your personal development, leading to an emotionally stronger, more adaptable, and ultimately smarter you!

Chapter 8

Physical Health: Strong Body, Strong Mind

" Take care of your body. It's the only place you have to live."

Jim Rohn

The Campus Lifestyle

Many may think, "Physical health? I've got this covered! I know to eat my fruits and veggies, hit the gym, and get some sleep." While that's a great start, college life can present unique challenges that may disrupt good intentions and overall well-being.

For many students, college marks their first experience living away from home and managing day-to-day life independently. This newfound freedom can be exhilarating; you determine when to study, socialize, eat, and organize your time. However, it can also be overwhelming, potentially causing physical health to take a back seat amid all the excitement. Late-night study sessions, unlimited meal plans, parties, and more can disrupt sleep patterns, dietary habits, and exercise routines. Living independently means taking greater responsibility for many aspects of life, and one of those crucial areas is physical health.

Staying healthy is not just about feeling good in your body but also about setting a foundation for the future. A healthy body supports a healthy mind, facilitating better focus on studies, improved stress management, and sustained energy levels. College life can often be hectic, with numerous academic and social demands. Being physically fit enables keeping up with these demands without burning out. Healthy habits are not just about surviving university years but also about thriving during and beyond them.

Moreover, alongside new college experiences come the pressure to stay on top of your studies. The workload is typically heavier than in high school, subjects are more challenging, and expectations are high. Academic stress, adjusting to a new social environment, and irregular sleep and eating patterns can all impact physical health. By acknowledging these, better choices can be made proactively to stay fit and flourish throughout college.

Lastly, it is essential to note that health is not only about the body; emotional wellness is also vital and can significantly influence overall well-being. As such, Chapter 9 is devoted to this subject to ensure it receives the detailed attention it deserves.

Nutrition & Hydration

Managing nutrition and hydration at college can be quite a maze. With a bustling cafeteria offering myriad food options, late-night pizza study breaks, and perhaps a vending machine run, making healthy choices is not always straightforward. However, what you eat and drink is incredibly important. Proper nutrition fuels the body, aiding better focus in class, increased energy levels, and a robust immune system. Good hydration is essential for staying refreshed, aiding digestion, and boosting mood.

Below, we consider healthy eating and drinking habits with practical tips for maintaining them amidst a busy college schedule. It is not about sticking to a strict diet or saying no to all your favorite treats. Instead, it is about balance and making choices that keep you feeling your best.

Essential Elements Of A Healthy Balanced Diet

A nutritious and balanced diet is vital as it supplies the body with essential nutrients to sustain health and vitality. Regular meals and healthy snacks throughout the day ensure a steady energy supply, enabling students to focus on studying and engaging in campus life.

Remember, it is all about balance! Perfect eating habits are not required, but minor changes can significantly impact overall well-being. Below are the primary components of a healthy diet.

Fruits & Vegetables: Incorporate these into meals to benefit from nature's superheroes; they are packed with fiber, vitamins, and minerals. Snacking on apples, bananas, or carrot sticks provides quick energy boosts.

Whole Grain Foods: Including whole wheat bread, oats, brown rice, and quinoa offers longer-lasting energy and promotes a feeling of fullness. Whole grains also provide essential nutrients for overall health.

Proteins: As the body's building blocks, proteins aid tissue repair and muscle strength. Sources include lean meats (chicken, turkey), fish, eggs, beans, lentils, tofu, and nuts.

Dairy Or Dairy Alternatives: Eating calcium-rich foods is crucial for strong bones. Yogurt, milk, and cheese serve as excellent sources of this nutrient. For those unable to consume dairy, fortified plant-based options like soy or almond milk are suitable alternatives.

Healthy Fats: Not all fats are bad! Healthy fats, like those found in avocados, seeds, nuts, and olive oil, benefit the brain and body.

Limit Sugar & Processed Foods: While indulging in sugary snacks, candies, and processed foods occasionally is okay, it is essential to minimize their intake. These items may provide a quick energy boost but often result in subsequent tiredness and low energy levels.

Allergies & Dietary Restrictions

Maintaining a healthy, balanced diet requires additional attention and careful consideration for students with allergies or dietary restrictions. Identifying and avoiding allergens or ingredients that trigger adverse reactions is critical.

Fortunately, numerous alternatives are usually available to ensure proper nutrition while accommodating specific dietary needs. For example, those with lactose intolerance can choose lactose-free or plant-based dairy alternatives. At the same time, those with gluten sensitivities can choose gluten-free whole grains like quinoa or brown rice. Additionally, incorporating a variety of fruits, vegetables, legumes, and protein sources such as tofu or nuts can help meet nutritional requirements while adhering to dietary restrictions.

Consult dietitians or healthcare professionals for advice on effectively navigating dietary challenges. By staying informed and making thoughtful choices, students with dietary restrictions or allergies can enjoy a diverse and nourishing diet conducive to overall health and well-being.

Stay Hydrated!

Drinking enough water may seem like a minor detail in the grand scheme of college life, but it is actually a vital component of overall well-being. Imagine the body as a well-oiled machine, and water is that essential lubricant. Without an adequate supply of water, various bodily functions begin to falter.

Individual hydration needs vary based on body size, activity level, climate, and overall health. Paying attention to thirst cues and maintaining a regular intake of fluids during the day is vital to meeting these needs.

The Brain: The human brain, comprising about 75% water, relies on hydration to function optimally. Dehydration can impair concentration and alertness, affecting performance, for example, in late-night study sessions and early-morning classes. Proper hydration is also crucial for cognitive function, memory retention, and mental clarity.

Muscles: Hydration is essential for maintaining optimal muscle function, whether engaging in rigorous physical activity or simply moving about. Insufficient water intake can lead to muscle soreness, cramping, or fatigue, even after adequate rest.

Digestion: Water is vital in aiding digestion, ensuring effective food processing, and preventing discomfort such as bloating. It facilitates the movement of food through the digestive tract and helps dissolve nutrients for absorption into the bloodstream.

Temperature Regulation: Water is critical in regulating body temperature, particularly during physical activity or exposure to hot environments. Sweating is the body's natural cooling mechanism, and adequate hydration is necessary to replace lost fluids and prevent overheating.

Electrolyte Balance: Electrolytes such as sodium, magnesium, and potassium are essential for fluid balance and supporting cellular function. Electrolyte-rich foods and beverages, such as sports drinks, can be beneficial during prolonged physical activity or excessive sweating.

Drink Water: Staying hydrated is relatively straightforward. Carry a refillable water bottle during the day, adding a slice of cucumber or lemon for a refreshing twist. Herbal tea and water-rich foods like fruits also contribute to hydration. So, before reaching for another cup of coffee during a study session, consider opting for water instead to keep your body functioning at its best.

Dining Hall Choices

Walking into the college dining hall can feel like entering a magical kingdom of unlimited food choices. With the array of options and the ability to eat as much as you want, making balanced and healthy choices can be challenging. Remember, it is not about being perfect but making small, sustainable choices that promote a healthier lifestyle.

Know Your Choices: Before grabbing a plate, walk around and check out all the food options available. There may be a salad bar, a sandwich station, a hot meal line, and a fruit section. Look out for dietary restrictions or allergy-friendly sections, which often cater to various dietary needs. Start planning your meal only after scoping out the available options.

A Balanced Plate: When choosing your food, aim for balance. Visualize the plate like a pie chart. Fill one quarter with lean proteins (like chicken, fish, tofu, or legumes), half with fruits or vegetables, and the rest with whole grains (like brown rice, whole grain pasta, or bread). This ensures a balanced and nutritious meal.

Portion Size Matters: While dining halls often allow unlimited food, portion sizes still matter. Start with smaller servings and wait a little before returning for seconds if necessary. This gives the brain time to register fullness and helps prevent overeating.

Healthy Swaps: Look for simple swaps to make meals more nutritious. For example, choose whole grain instead of white bread, grilled chicken over fried options, or water or unsweetened iced tea instead of sugary drinks.

Listen To Your Body: Pay attention to your body's hunger and fullness cues. Eat only when genuinely hungry, and stop when satisfied, even if food remains on the plate. Also, avoid eating simply because it is a designated mealtime or because others are eating.

Common Nutritional Pitfalls

Amidst the whirlwind of classes, social events, and newfound independence, it is easy to fall into bad eating habits. A healthy, balanced diet can be maintained by being aware of these dangers and making minor changes to eating habits. Below are common examples and tips on how to avoid them.

Skipping Meals: Whether you're running late for class or engrossed in studying, skipping a meal can lead to excessive hunger later, often resulting in overeating or less healthy options. Aim to have at least three balanced meals daily, and remember that even a quick snack like fruit or nuts can help keep hunger at bay.

Too Much Junk Food: With vending machines and fast-food delivery at your fingertips, it is tempting to rely on high-fat, high-sugar, and high-salt options. However, these foods lack the nutrients for sustained energy and overall health. While enjoying these treats occasionally is fine, strive to balance them with more nutritious choices.

Overdoing The Caffeine: Falling into the caffeine trap is common during late-night study sessions. While coffee or energy drinks may seem like quick fixes for staying awake, excessive caffeine intake can lead to jitteriness, disrupted sleep, and headaches. Limiting caffeine and considering alternatives like water, herbal tea, or a short nap to boost energy can be beneficial.

Not Enough Fruits & Veggies: It is common to forget to include enough fruits and vegetables. These foods are rich in vital minerals and vitamins for optimal body function. Make it a habit to include a portion of fruits or veggies in each meal, and remember that frozen and canned options are convenient alternatives.

Be Sensible, Not Obsessive On Healthy Eating

While maintaining a nutritious diet is essential for overall health, it is equally crucial to avoid becoming fixated on healthy eating. Enjoying occasional treats or favorite foods is a normal part of a balanced diet. Obsessive behaviors around food can lead to the development of eating disorders, which can have severe consequences on both physical and mental well-being. It can inadvertently contribute to an unhealthy relationship with food, as well as anxiety and stress. When preoccupation with food, body image, or guilt about eating interferes with well-being, seeking support from a healthcare professional may be necessary. Professionals such as dietitians, counselors, and mental health specialists can offer guidance to cultivate a healthier relationship with food and body image. Remember, health encompasses both physical and psychological well-being; neglecting one for the sake of the other is counterproductive.

While nutrition and hydration are vital aspects of health, they should not overshadow the joy of eating or lead to negative self-perception. Embracing a balanced approach to food is vital for overall health and happiness.

For more aspects of achieving a balanced diet, head over to Chapter 10. There, we explore how to eat healthily from a practical angle, including cooking techniques, food safety practices, and budget-friendly meals.

Exercise & Physical Activity

Finding time to exercise might be challenging amidst academic demands, social activities, and perhaps a part-time job. However, staying active is essential for overall physical health and well-being.

Regular exercise offers numerous benefits beyond just physical fitness. It helps to manage stress, boosts mood, increases energy levels, and promotes better sleep. Also, keeping a healthy weight is crucial as it lowers the risk of health conditions such as heart disease, high blood pressure, and diabetes.

While skipping the gym for extra study time or sleep may seem tempting or necessary, remember that exercise enhances academic performance and overall well-being. Every bit of movement counts, so starting small is perfectly fine. As stamina improves and fun activities are discovered, exercise becomes integral to the college routine. So, grab your sneakers and get moving!

Find What Works for You

Discovering enjoyable activities helps to maintain a regular exercise routine. While "exercise" may evoke images of monotonous treadmill runs or grueling weightlifting sessions, it can encompass many other activities. It could be a dance class, yoga, swimming, or a stroll around campus. Finding something suitable and enjoyable is key. Aim for a mix of cardio activities such as running or cycling, strength training like lifting weights, and flexibility exercises such as yoga or stretching throughout the week.

Campus Fitness Opportunities

College often provides many sports and exercise options, catering to various interests and fitness levels. There is something for everyone, from usual options such as basketball, soccer, and volleyball to less common activities such as rock climbing, ultimate frisbee, or even quidditch.

Additionally, many colleges provide access to state-of-the-art fitness facilities, group exercise classes, and intramural leagues, allowing students to explore and try new activities. Embracing these opportunities not only promotes physical health but also fosters camaraderie, stress relief, and personal growth. So, go and try something new – you might discover a passion you never knew existed!

Incorporate Into Your Routine

One strategy for fitting exercise into a busy schedule is to make it a routine. Schedule workouts at a consistent time each day, even if it is just a 15-minute walk between classes. Every bit of physical activity adds up.

Another way is to get involved in on-campus activities. Good options include joining a sports team, finding a workout buddy, or taking a fitness class to stay motivated. Consider active ways of getting around campus, like cycling instead of taking the bus or driving.

Utilize Technology

Technology can be a powerful ally in staying fit. Fitness trackers (including smartwatches or fitness bands) monitor steps, measure distances walked or run, and track heart rate. These devices often sync with smartphone apps to provide a comprehensive overview of activity levels and progress.

Fitness apps can offer workout suggestions, meal plans, and tools to track sleep patterns. Some apps even make the fitness experience more social, turning it into a fun challenge with friends rather than a chore. With many options available, individuals will likely find one that aligns with their needs and preferences.

Importance Of Sleep

Sleep is necessary for optimal physical health and mental well-being, especially amidst the demands of college life.

Why Sleep Is Vital

Sleep is fundamental and extends beyond merely resting the body. During sleep, the body undergoes a comprehensive rejuvenation process, including tissue repair, hormone production, and memory consolidation. Adequate sleep is thus vital for physical health, cognitive function, and emotional well-being.

Persistent sleep deprivation can have severe consequences. It can contribute to weight gain, compromise the immune system, and increase the risk of conditions including heart disease and diabetes. Insufficient sleep can also impact mood, leading to irritability, anxiety, or depression while hindering cognitive performance necessary for academic success.

Maintain A Healthy Sleep Schedule

Establishing a consistent sleep routine is vital to ensuring adequate rest. Try to keep a consistent routine by going to sleep and waking up at the same time every day, even on weekends. This helps regulate the body's internal clock, making falling asleep and waking up easier.

Additionally, incorporating a relaxing pre-sleep routine can promote better sleep quality. Activities such as reading, bathing, or listening to soothing music can help settle the mind and body for sleep.

Don't Use Screens Before Sleeping

Avoid screen use before bedtime. The blue light emitted by these devices suppresses the production of melatonin, a hormone that regulates sleep. The light disrupts the body's natural sleep-wake cycle, reducing sleep quality and making it harder to fall asleep.

Common Sleep Issues In College

College life presents challenges to maintaining ideal sleep habits. Factors such as late-night roommates, social events, and all-night study sessions for exams can disrupt sleep patterns. Strategies like earplugs or a white noise machine can help manage noise disturbances, while studying in a well-lit area and avoiding working in bed can preserve the association between bed and sleep.

Excessive caffeine consumption during the day poses another obstacle to quality sleep. Avoid coffee intake at least six hours before bedtime to allow the stimulant effects to wear off. Know that caffeine is also present in tea, chocolate, sodas, and certain medications, so consider reducing intake, especially closer to bedtime.

While occasional sleep disturbances are common, persistent difficulties falling asleep, staying asleep, or experiencing chronic fatigue despite sufficient rest may warrant seeking help from healthcare professionals. It is crucial to take sleep seriously. Like a balanced diet and regular exercise, good sleep is essential for good health.

Alcohol, Tobacco & Substance Use

Legal Age For Alcohol & Tobacco: In the US, the legal age to purchase and consume alcohol and tobacco products is 21 (students outside the US should check with their local legal requirements in this respect). These age restrictions are federally mandated and strictly enforced across college campuses. Violating these laws can result in academic disciplinary measures and legal consequences. Understanding and following these legal requirements is crucial for the safety and well-being of all students.

The Real College Scene: Despite the minimum age for buying and consuming alcohol and tobacco being 21, the reality is that these and other illicit substances are often present in the college environment. While exploring new experiences is part of college life, it is vital to recognize the impact that alcohol, tobacco, and illegal drugs can have on overall health. Remember, every person has the right to decline participation in any activity they are uncomfortable with. Responsible decision-making concerning these substances is critical.

Alcohol & Health: Alcohol often plays a role in college social life. While moderate drinking may fit into a balanced lifestyle for those of legal age, excessive drinking can lead to a host of health issues, from immediate risks such as accidents or alcohol poisoning to long-term effects like liver disease or addiction. Additionally, alcoholic beverages can lead to weight gain as these are often high in calories and can increase hunger.

Know Your Limits: Responsible alcohol consumption is essential. This means understanding limits, drinking slowly, and never drinking on an empty stomach. Always tell a trusted friend your whereabouts and remember that it is entirely acceptable to abstain from alcohol.

Substance Abuse: Illicit drugs and the misuse of prescription medications are hazardous to physical and mental health. These substances are highly addictive and can result in significant harm, including damage to vital organs and the development of mental health disorders. Using drugs to cope with stress or other life challenges is neither healthy nor sustainable.

Consequences: Alcohol and drug use can have severe consequences, impacting both mental and physical well-being. It can impair judgment, leading to lower inhibitions and risky behavior such as aggression and unsafe sexual activities. When under the influence, a person may act out of character, contradict their values, or make comments they later regret. In addition to damaged reputation and strained relationships, it can lead to legal issues, academic failure, and mental health disorders such as anxiety or depression. It is, therefore, crucial for students to appreciate these risks and make informed choices regarding alcohol and substance use.

Tobacco & Health: Tobacco use is a significant risk for numerous health conditions, including heart disease, stroke, and a variety of cancers. Second-hand smoke also poses health risks to others. For those who smoke and are considering quitting, numerous resources are available to support this decision.

Be Informed & Seek Help If Needed: Navigating these issues can be challenging. Colleges provide various resources, such as counseling services, peer support groups, and educational workshops, for those facing pressure or struggling with substance use. Seeking support is a wise and courageous step, and engaging with healthcare professionals for healthier coping strategies is vital for long-term well-being.

Sickness

Living in close quarters in dormitories, attending packed lecture halls, socializing at events, and dining in crowded areas are all common occurrences in college life. Unfortunately, they are also major contributors to the quick and easy spread of common illnesses. Additionally, the stress and lack of sleep that often comes with demanding study schedules and social events can further weaken the immune system's defenses.

Common Illnesses In College

Colds & Flu: Symptoms include coughing, sneezing, and fever.

Stomach Bugs: Contagious gastrointestinal viruses, such as norovirus, often result in stomach upset, vomiting, and diarrhea and spread through contaminated food or surfaces.

Mononucleosis ("Mono"): Known as the "kissing disease," this is caused by the Epstein-Barr virus and is characterized by fatigue, a sore throat, and fever.

Skin Infections: Conditions such as ringworm, athlete's foot, and impetigo can spread through skin-to-skin contact or shared items.

Respiratory Illnesses: These refer to infections such as bronchitis and pneumonia that can lead to symptoms like coughing and difficulty breathing.

Conjunctivitis (Pink Eye): This eye infection can cause redness, irritation, and discharge from the eyes.

Herpes Simplex (Cold Sores): These are triggered by the Herpes Simplex Virus and spread by physical contact or sharing items such as utensils or lip balm. Symptoms start with a tingling sensation around the lips or mouth, followed by the appearance of small fluid-filled blisters.

Preventing & Managing Sickness

Coping with being sick while at college can be tough, especially when away from home. However, these situations can be effectively managed with proactive measures, self-care during illness, and seeking assistance when needed.

The following offers basic guidance for addressing common illnesses. Please note that this information does not constitute medical advice and should not replace professional medical consultation. Health conditions vary; what works for one person may not apply to another. When experiencing illness, especially severe or persistent symptoms, seeking prompt medical attention is crucial. College health centers or local healthcare providers can provide personalized care and recommendations tailored to individual needs.

Practice Proper Hygiene: Prevention and maintaining basic hygiene practices are essential. Regular handwashing, particularly before meals and after using the restroom, can considerably reduce the risk of illness. Hand sanitizer is also effective when soap and water are not available. Keeping living spaces clean and avoiding the sharing of personal items such as towels or eating utensils can further prevent the spread of germs.

Stay Healthy: Prioritize activities that support overall health, including regular exercise, eating a nutritious diet, and ensuring an adequate amount of sleep. These practices strengthen the immune system and enhance resilience against illness.

Inoculations: Many colleges offer vaccinations, such as flu shots, which protect against specific diseases.

Self-Care: Despite preventive efforts, illness may still occur. If feeling unwell, focus on rest, adequate sleep, hydration, and eating nutritious foods, which are essential for the body's healing process. Over-the-counter medicines can sometimes alleviate certain symptoms, but following the dosage instructions on the label is necessary.

Persistent Symptoms: If symptoms persist or become severe, medical assistance is essential. College healthcare providers should be able to diagnose, treat, and guide recovery and prevent the spread of illness.

Inform Academic Staff: Notify relevant professors promptly of any absences due to illness. Most are understanding and can offer options for making up for missed coursework or exams.

Injury Prevention & First Aid

Navigating campus life presents various opportunities for injury, whether through sports, daily activities, or simply moving around. Sprains and strains from the overstretching or tearing of ligaments, muscles, or tendons are common during physical activities. Fractures and dislocations may arise from accidents or participation in high-impact sports. Cuts and abrasions frequently occur from everyday activities like cooking or handling sharp objects, and repetitive strain injuries develop over time from continuous repetitive motion. Burns are common and often happen in the kitchen or from contact with hot objects.

Injury Prevention

Despite these injury risks, proactive steps can be taken to lower these risks.

Exercise Safety: Adequate preparation is vital to injury-free physical activity. To prepare the muscles, always begin with a warm-up and end with a cool-down. Using the correct equipment and mastering the proper techniques are essential in preventing sports-related injuries.

Walking & Cycling: Many students walk or bike around campus, so awareness of the environment and adherence to safety rules is vital. Use sidewalks and bike lanes, wear reflective attire, and use lights after dark to maintain visibility.

Fall Prevention: Keep living spaces orderly to prevent tripping hazards. Exercise caution on bunk beds and where floors may be slippery, such as after rain or in icy conditions. Additionally, be mindful of wet floors in communal areas, especially in showers and baths, and clean up spillages immediately to avoid slips and falls.

Avoid Repetitive Strain Injuries (RSI): Repetitive motions, especially during activities like typing, can lead to RSIs. Applying the 20-20-20 rule - every 20 minutes, take a 20-second break to look at something 20 feet away - can mitigate this risk. This practice benefits the hands and wrists as well as the eyes. Ergonomic accessories for computers and maintaining neutral wrist positions can further aid in preventing these injuries.

A Proper Posture: Maintaining good posture is critical to avoid back, neck, and shoulder pain. Long hours spent over books or a laptop can strain these areas. An ergonomic setup supports proper alignment and lowers the risk of discomfort or RSIs. Good posture means sitting with a straight back, relaxed shoulders, and both feet flat on the floor.

First Aid Essentials

Accidents can still occur despite taking preventative measures, and being prepared can help manage such situations. Here are some general guidelines for basic first aid and preparedness.

Sprains & Strains: Use the "RICE" method: **R**est the affected area, **I**ce it for 20 minutes periodically, **C**ompress with a bandage (not too tight), and **E**levate above the heart to reduce swelling and speed recovery.

Suspected Fractures Or Dislocations: Immobilize the area and seek immediate medical attention.

Concussions: Monitor the individual for signs of confusion or unconsciousness and get medical help.

Minor Cuts & Abrasions: Clean the wound, apply pressure to stop the bleeding, then cover it with a sterile bandage.

RSI: Take breaks to rest the affected area, and use ice or heat as recommended. If pain persists, consult a healthcare provider.

Minor Burns: Cool the burn immediately under cold, gentle running water, then cover with a clean, dry cloth. For more severe burns or burns caused by chemicals, it is essential to seek medical attention immediately.

First Aid Kit: Keep one in the dorm with essentials like band-aids, antiseptic wipes, tweezers, medical tape, a digital thermometer, and pain relievers.

CPR & First Aid Training: Consider acquiring skills to manage emergencies by becoming CPR and first aid certified through courses offered at many colleges.

Seek Medical Attention: For severe injuries or if in doubt, seek professional medical attention promptly. Know the location of the nearest hospital and have the campus health center's contact information accessible.

Disclaimer: The advice offered is only intended as general information and must not be considered a replacement for seeking professional medical advice. Always seek guidance from healthcare professionals for all medical concerns or injuries, as they can provide tailored advice based on individual circumstances. Furthermore, while the following tips on basic first aid can be beneficial in many circumstances, they may not be appropriate for all injuries or emergencies. It is essential to evaluate each situation carefully and prioritize safety above everything else.

Understanding Healthcare Services

While basic first aid knowledge is essential for immediate and minor injuries, it's also crucial for students to understand their healthcare options for peace of mind should the need arise.

Insurance Requirements: Many US colleges require students to have health insurance, and often offer a student health plan covering medical care ranging from regular doctor's appointments to emergency room visits and specialist consultations. It's essential to understand the plan's details, including enrollment procedures, payment processes, coverage benefits, and how to file claims. For students in other countries, healthcare requirements can vary; some have government healthcare programs, while others may require private insurance.

Local Registration: Students outside the US may need to register with a local clinic or general practitioner before accessing healthcare services.

Campus Health Services: Many colleges provide on-campus clinics that offer primary care, mental health support, and, in some cases, emergency medical services.

Local Facilities & Emergency Preparedness: Knowing the locations of healthcare providers, including clinics, hospitals, or specialized student health services, is useful. Awareness of the nearest hospital's Emergency Room (ER) for urgent care is crucial.

Hygiene & Personal Care

A robust routine in personal hygiene and cleanliness is vital for promoting health and well-being in college. The below guidelines are a starting point, and students are encouraged to adapt their care routines to their specific needs and seek advice from healthcare professionals when necessary.

Room Cleanliness: Regularly clean surfaces like desks, keyboards, and doorknobs to maintain a healthy environment. A tidy and clutter-free dorm room supports health and creates a conducive environment for study and relaxation.

Good Hygiene: More than just about appearance, good hygiene is vital for staying healthy and preventing disease. Along with regular bathing and frequent handwashing, keeping hair and nails clean and trimmed can curb the spread of infections. Good hygiene also boosts self-confidence and comfort around others.

Beware Of Sharing: The communal nature of dorm living increases the risk of skin infections. Avoid sharing personal items, including towels, razors, or makeup. Regularly clean items that touch the face, such as phones and glasses, to prevent bacteria from spreading. Disinfect gym equipment before and after use, and wear flip-flops in communal showers to prevent common fungal infections.

Wash Clothes Often: Regularly laundering clothes, bedding, and towels prevent bacterial growth. Avoid letting laundry pile up and after washing, ensure thorough drying to ward off mold and mildew.

Oral Health: A comprehensive oral hygiene routine is fundamental, including brushing teeth twice daily and flossing. Along with limiting sugary and starchy snacks and drinks, consider using an electric toothbrush for thorough cleaning and mouthwash for fresh breath and to eliminate remaining bacteria. Frequent dental visits for check-ups and professional cleanings are crucial for preventing dental problems.

Eye Health: Given the extensive use of digital screens, maintaining eye health is more important than ever. Regular eye check-ups, following the 20-20-20 rule to rest the eyes, and practicing proper screen ergonomics, such as reducing glare, can help preserve vision and prevent strain.

Ergonomics For Students

Ergonomics, the study of designing workspaces to suit the user's needs, is essential for students who dedicate considerable time to studying or computer work. Improper setup can lead to discomfort and potentially long-term health problems.

Creating An Ergonomic Study Space

This can be both simple and economical to set up. Chairs and desks should be adjusted so that the knees are at or below hip level when seated and the feet rest flat on the floor. The computer screen should ideally be positioned at eye level, allowing a straight or slightly downward gaze, minimizing neck and upper back strain. Keyboards must be set up to ensure that shoulders stay relaxed, elbows are somewhat open, and wrists and hands remain straight along the forearm line.

Incorporating ergonomic tools, such as adjustable chairs, can enhance posture support if budget allows. Ergonomic keyboards and mice can lessen the strain on wrists and hands, which is beneficial during prolonged study sessions. Laptop stands or monitor risers are advisable to raise screens to eye level, preventing excessive neck bending. While these tools are aids to physical health, maintaining a proper posture and taking frequent breaks are equally, if not more, important.

Prioritizing ergonomics and good posture are an investment in one's physical well-being, making studying more comfortable and promoting well-being in the long term.

Impact Of Stress On Physical Health

The demands of college life, such as academic responsibilities, extracurricular activities, and social engagements, can often lead to stress. Effectively recognizing and managing stress is critical for optimal health and well-being.

Recognize Physical Signs Of Stress: When stressed, the body releases hormones that accelerate the heartbeat and tighten muscles. These short-term reactions are normal, but if stress becomes prolonged, it can lead to more severe health problems such as heart disease, diabetes, elevated blood pressure, and the worsening of conditions like asthma. Common physical symptoms of stress include headaches, digestive disturbances, chest pain, and sleep problems. Unaddressed, stress can lead to mental health conditions like depression and anxiety. Early recognition of these signs and implementing stress management techniques are critical to prevent adverse health impacts.

The Physical-Mental Health Connection: Physical well-being is closely tied to mental health. Chronic physical illnesses can induce mental health challenges, and conversely, mental health issues can take a toll on the body. To support mental health, it is essential to maintain physical health through consistent exercise, a nourishing diet, and adequate sleep.

The Impact Of Friendships: The quality of relationships formed in college can significantly affect physical health. Positive relationships can provide crucial support in stressful times, while negative or toxic interactions can increase stress and adversely impact health. Cultivating supportive relationships and seeking help when facing challenges is key to managing stress effectively.

Balancing Studying & Health: Striking a healthy balance between academic duties and physical self-care is essential. Excessive focus on studies at the expense of physical health can lead to burnout. Exercise, a balanced nutritious diet, and adequate sleep are fundamental for maintaining health and academic performance.

How To Manage Stress

Controlling stress is essential for maintaining physical health and well-being. Below is a recap of strategies that can be instrumental in managing or reducing stress, especially when integrating these strategies into daily life.

Staying Active: Physical activity is an effective stress reducer. It prompts the body to release endorphins, also known as "feel-good hormones." These can improve mood and act as natural stress relievers. Regular exercise also promotes better sleep and improved self-esteem.

Eating Well: Nutrition plays a crucial role in stress management. Diets high in caffeine or sugar can exacerbate anxiety, while a diet abundant in lean proteins, fruits, vegetables, and whole grains can fortify the body against the effects of stress.

Ensuring Adequate Sleep: Insufficient sleep can amplify stress and anxiety. Strive for 7 to 9 hours of restful sleep per night, tailored to individual needs. A regular sleep schedule and a peaceful environment are conducive to improved sleep quality. Reducing screen time before going to bed is also beneficial.

Practicing Relaxation Techniques: Physical relaxation practices can reduce muscle tension and lower blood pressure. Techniques such as meditation, deep breathing, yoga, or tai chi can foster calmness and decrease stress levels. Including at least one of these practices in daily life can be beneficial.

Leaning On Friends: A robust social support network can be a powerful asset in managing stress. Sharing concerns with friends and family can provide solace and a different perspective during stressful times.

Mastering Time Management: Organizing time effectively can alleviate stress, particularly from academic or occupational demands. Structuring tasks, prioritizing effectively, and allowing time for regular breaks can help maintain control over a busy schedule.

Prioritizing physical health and well-being is vital during college and beyond. A balanced diet, sufficient hydration, regular exercise, adequate sleep, and effective stress management are key components. Personal hygiene, injury prevention, and routine health check-ups, including dental and vision, are also essential for overall wellness.

College life extends beyond studying and getting good grades; it's also about learning to balance different life aspects, including health. A strong and healthy body not only supports academic success but also enhances your overall college experience. The healthy habits you establish now will lay the groundwork for lifelong well-being.

Maintaining your health is ongoing, and setbacks are a part of the process. What's important is your continued effort and ability to adjust. With this understanding, you can make informed choices and take charge of your well-being, one step at a time.

CHAPTER 9

STRESS LESS, THRIVE MORE

" You have power over your mind, not outside events.
Realize this, and you will find strength."

Marcus Aurelius

Amidst the rush of settling into new college life, it is essential not to overlook a vital aspect of your well-being - emotional and mental health. This encompasses how we think, feel, and behave and influences our ability to handle stress, form relationships, and make decisions. Good mental health extends beyond the lack of depression, anxiety, or other psychological issues; it encompasses positive characteristics such as coping with life's challenges, having a sense of purpose, managing stress, bouncing back from adversity, and enjoying life.

This chapter aims to provide a deeper understanding of emotional and mental well-being. We'll explore topics from understanding emotional health to recognizing common challenges faced in college, together with strategies for managing stress and achieving a balanced lifestyle.

Remember, experiencing ups and downs is normal, and seeking help is acceptable when facing struggles. College is not solely about academic growth but also personal maturity and self-discovery. So, let's delve into understanding and implementing strategies to nurture a healthier, happier, and emotionally stronger you.

What Is Emotional & Mental Health?

Emotional and mental health are closely related yet distinct components contributing to one's overall well-being. It is essential to recognize their differences and be able to address any issues with either of them appropriately.

Emotional Health: This is the capacity to acknowledge, understand, and control emotions effectively. It involves identifying and expressing emotions, including happiness, sadness, anger, and love. Emotional health also entails handling stress, adapting to changes, and forming healthy relationships.

Mental Health: This is a broader, more comprehensive term that encompasses psychological, emotional, and social well-being. It entails thinking, learning, and reasoning effectively and forming and sustaining positive relationships with others. Moreover, mental health includes the capability to cope with life's challenges, effectively manage stress and anxiety, and maintain a sense of purpose and fulfillment. A sound mental state is vital for overall well-being and personal development.

In summary, emotional health focuses on feelings, while mental health covers a broader spectrum of cognitive and social skills.

Common Challenges

College life comes with its own set of challenges and opportunities. Students face academic pressures, the need to forge new friendships, the experience of living away from home, and adjusting to a new environment. All these contribute to a potentially stressful and challenging period. Therefore, prioritizing emotional and mental well-being during this time is imperative, given its impact on stress management, academic achievement, and the overall college experience. Below, we will explore common issues frequently encountered by students and coping strategies to overcome them. Please be reassured and remember that you are not alone in facing these challenges.

Academic Pressure

College presents challenges with high expectations and the pressure to excel. The stress of exams, coursework, and extracurricular activities can feel like carrying a heavy load. This pressure may result in procrastination and difficulty concentrating on studying. Unchecked, ongoing stress and worry can lead to burnout, loss of interest, and difficulty fulfilling responsibilities.

Managing this academic pressure involves simple strategies such as organization and effective studying with SMART goals. These concepts were covered earlier in Chapter 4, "Study Smarter, Not Harder." Strategies specifically relating to mental well-being are summarized below.

Time Management Strategies: Planning the week helps understand tasks and their deadlines. Using a planner or digital calendar assists in tracking assignments and other responsibilities. Additionally, incorporating breaks for relaxation and enjoyment is equally essential. Maintaining flexibility in the schedule is also practical to allow for unexpected events, such as last-minute social gatherings or emergencies. This flexibility enables adaptation to changing circumstances without sacrificing overall productivity and well-being.

Set Realistic Goals & Expectations: Aiming high is commendable, but setting unrealistic goals can lead to unnecessary stress. It is essential to be honest with yourself about achievable objectives. Accept that perfection is not necessary, and that grades or achievements do not solely define your worth. Divide large tasks into smaller, more manageable portions, and celebrate each step of progress along the way.

Maintain A Healthy Balance: Getting caught up in studying and assignments is easy, but also pay attention to your health. Make time to relax and recharge with activities like reading, walking, or socializing. Ensure good nutrition, adequate sleep, and regular exercise. A balanced schedule supports both mental well-being and academic success.

Homesickness & Loneliness

It is common to feel homesick and lonely, especially if it is the first time living away from home. Feelings of isolation and missing the familiarity and comforts of home can impact emotional health.

Create A Homely Environment: Consider decorating your room with items that bring happy memories or establish comforting routines like those back home. Also, keeping contact with home friends and family is vital. Regular phone calls, video chats or even writing letters can help bridge the distance and keep a sense of connection. Remember, making new friends in college does not mean having to lose touch with home.

Be Patient – Give It Time: Homesickness is natural and reflects deep connections and affection for home and loved ones. Allow time to settle in and adapt to new surroundings; there is no rush to overcome these feelings overnight. Instead, acknowledge and face them without fear. With time, these feelings will improve.

Get Immersed In College Life: Engage in activities such as joining clubs, participating in campus events, or exploring the new city. Keeping busy and making new friends can distract you from homesickness and help you develop a new sense of belonging.

If homesickness significantly impacts daily life, do not hesitate to seek support. Most college campuses offer counseling services that can provide practical strategies to assist with this transition.

Depression

Depression is not merely feeling down or having a bad day occasionally; it is a real and serious condition that profoundly impacts how one feels, thinks, and acts. It can feel like a heavy, persistent cloud that refuses to lift. Symptoms may include persistent sadness or emptiness lasting over a few weeks, which can interfere with studies, social life, and daily activities. Changes in sleep patterns, loss of interest in previously enjoyable activities, appetite changes, and negative thoughts are also common signs.

Recognizing these signs in yourself or a friend is crucial. Overcoming depression is not easily achieved through sheer willpower alone, but the good news is that it is treatable. Many colleges provide mental health services with professionals trained to assist in navigating these feelings and finding coping strategies. Seeking help is a brave first step towards feeling better. Remember, you are not alone, and there is no shame in asking for help.

Stress & Anxiety

Stress and anxiety are distinct yet commonly encountered emotions. Stress often arises from specific pressures, such as upcoming exams or moving to a new area, and typically diminishes after the situation is resolved. In contrast, anxiety may persist even without clear reasons, continuing even in seemingly calm conditions. Both can cause significant discomfort and require various coping strategies.

Acknowledge, Identify & Address

When faced with stress or anxiety, it is crucial first to acknowledge and be aware of these feelings. Next, identifying the root causes is essential, as this understanding allows for assessing appropriate actions to address the situation. For example, when academic and social commitments become overwhelming, adopting smart study habits and improving time management can make a significant difference. Similarly, in the case of personal conflicts with friends, partners, or roommates, addressing and proactively working through these issues to resolve them is advisable rather than letting them persist.

Causes: For students, stress often originates from heavy workloads, high academic expectations, a new environment, forming friendships, or concerns about the future. Anxiety, which may accompany stress, often stems from worrying about these same issues and other facets of life.

Symptoms: Stress and anxiety can profoundly impact students emotionally and physically. Emotionally, an ongoing sense of unease or worry may lack a specific trigger. Enjoyment in previously liked activities or social events may wane, leading to avoidance. Physically, there may be restlessness, faster heartbeat, headaches, disturbed sleep, or changes in eating habits. These symptoms can interfere with concentration, hinder studying, and complicate social interactions.

Pinpointing the cause of stress and anxiety enables the determination and implementation of the best course of action. Proactively addressing concerns helps restore control over one's emotions, providing a sense of empowerment, even when immediate resolutions are not apparent.

Healthy Habits For Emotional & Mental Well-Being

The state of the body and mind are inextricably entwined, so strategies promoting physical fitness are also relevant to mental well-being. For a detailed discussion of these, please refer to Chapter 8 on Physical Health. Below is a summary of approaches pertinent to mental well-being.

Regular Exercise & Activity: Physical activity benefits the body and the mind. Exercise can alleviate feelings of anxiety and enhance mood. Strive to be active for at least 30 minutes every day.

Balanced Nutrition: A well-balanced diet provides essential nutrients to fuel both the body and mind. Avoid excessive sugar or junk food, as they can result in energy crashes and mood fluctuations.

Adequate Sleep: This is crucial for emotional and cognitive functions. Sufficient sleep supports better thinking, decision-making, and stress management. Most adults require 7 to 9 hours of sleep each night. A consistent bedtime and relaxing routine can promote better sleep quality.

Mental Strength & Resilience

Being mentally strong is not about never having problems; it is about learning how to handle them and bounce back from challenges when they arise. Resilience is a quality that can be developed by adjusting one's mindset and approach during tough times.

Developing Coping Skills

College life can be like a rollercoaster ride with highs and lows, from demanding classes to interpersonal conflicts, and stress is sometimes inevitable.

Effective coping strategies enhance the ability to overcome obstacles. While it may be tempting to suppress emotions or avoid challenging situations, consistently utilizing these skills results in greater resilience. Think of it as building a safety net; equipped with these tools, you are better prepared to face whatever comes your way.

Stress Management Techniques

Techniques to manage emotional and mental health challenges are necessary to help regain a sense of balance and well-being. These practices should not be seen as standalone solutions but complementary to proactive problem-solving. They can provide comfort and perspective when things do not go as planned. Note that each person will have their preferred coping mechanisms that help restore equilibrium and calmness.

Breathing: When the body is stressed, the heart rate increases, and breaths become shorter and faster. To counteract this, clear the mind, close the eyes, take slow, deep breaths, and concentrate on the inhalation and exhalation process. Deep breathing for a few minutes can help bring the body back to a more relaxed level from an elevated, stressed, or anxious state.

Mindfulness: This is about staying fully present in the current moment. Rather than stressing about the future or dwelling on the past, focus on what is happening now. This could be as simple as paying attention to the sensation of your feet on the ground, the taste of food, or the sound of your breath. Both deep breathing and mindfulness can help lower stress and bring a sense of calm and peace.

Expressing Emotions: Occasionally, feelings are kept bottled up, leading to heightened stress and anxiety. It is crucial to find a suitable outlet for these emotions. This could be confiding in a trusted friend or counselor, or conveying feelings through creative outlets, such as drawing, painting, or playing a musical instrument. Expressing emotions allows for acknowledgment and a better understanding of these issues. This, in turn, can translate to better emotional management and overall mental well-being.

Journaling: This involves regularly writing down thoughts and feelings or doing so during difficult periods. This practice helps understand emotions better, notice patterns or triggers, and reflect on experiences. Entries can be brief or detailed. Reflecting on past writings during challenging times can serve as a reminder of progress and improvement. Essentially, putting thoughts and feelings into words can be therapeutic and beneficial.

Using Apps: In today's digital world, students can find great value in using apps to alleviate stress and anxiety. These apps provide a convenient way to manage emotions and mental well-being by providing guided meditation, deep-breathing exercises, and cognitive-behavioral therapy techniques. With features like mood tracking, relaxation exercises, and mindfulness practices, these apps can be tailored to meet specific needs and preferences. Additionally, many offer round-the-clock support, allowing access to guidance whenever and wherever needed.

Develop A Support Network

Having a solid support network is crucial when facing emotional and mental health challenges. Friends and family can provide support, encouragement, and valuable perspective. Do not hesitate to reach out to them when feeling stressed or down. Additionally, college campuses often offer resources such as counseling services, peer support groups, or stress and anxiety management workshops.

Seek Professional Help

Sometimes, seeking professional support can be a more practical option than self-care, coping techniques, or encouragement from loved ones. It can also offer greater privacy and confidentiality. Looking after one's mental well-being is as crucial as looking after physical health. Just as one would consult a doctor for an illness, mental health is the same and should be given equal attention and care.

Counselors & Mental Health Professionals: They are experts in supporting individuals facing emotional and mental health challenges. They offer valuable insights into what one may be experiencing and suggest effective coping strategies and ways to navigate difficult experiences. They also create a safe and supportive setting to express emotions without judgment. Instead of being critical, their approach is focused on providing support and guidance.

Overcoming The Stigma Of Seeking Help: Students may feel embarrassed doing this, but there is no need to. Asking for help is a positive step and a sign of strength, not weakness. Recognizing a problem and taking action is courageous and requires determination.

How To Access Campus Mental Health Services: Colleges typically provide resources for student mental health, such as counseling, peer support groups, or stress management workshops. Information about these services can usually be found on the college's website, through inquiries with a trusted professor, or by visiting the student health center. It is normal to feel hesitant about seeking help; however, remember that these resources are there to support you.

Teletherapy: Also known as online counseling, this can be an excellent alternative for those who feel that campus services are insufficient, have a busy schedule, or prefer more privacy. With various digital platforms, students can connect with licensed professionals and communicate through messages, phone, or video, all from the comfort of their own private space. However, it is essential to verify the service's credibility, understand the privacy policies, and ensure that the counselor has the necessary qualifications and experience.

Learn To Recover After Setbacks

Building resilience is about learning to get back up each time life knocks you down. Feeling upset or disappointed when circumstances don't go as planned is normal, but resilience means not staying down. Instead, it is about learning from setbacks, dusting yourself off, and moving forward. Maintaining a positive mindset is vital. Try to see challenges not as roadblocks but as opportunities for growth.

Maintaining perspective is also crucial. View setbacks as temporary hurdles, not as defining moments. Remember also that good nutrition, regular exercise, and enough sleep can all boost resilience.

Be Kind To Yourself

It is natural to be self-critical when situations do not go as planned. However, showing kindness and giving yourself a break can be more beneficial. Think of it as how you would support a friend in a similar situation - with understanding and encouragement. Extend that same compassion to yourself. Instead of dwelling on mistakes, recognize that everyone falters sometimes; it is part of being human.

Positive self-talk also plays a role in building resilience. Words can significantly influence our emotions, so speaking to ourselves with positivity and encouragement is helpful.

When negative thoughts arise - pause and reframe. Rather than saying, "I'm terrible at this," remind yourself that challenges are temporary, and you are doing your best. Instead, say "I'm having a tough time, but I'm resilient, and I will overcome this." The shift to positive self-talk fosters resilience and self-belief, empowering you to persevere and grow stronger.

So, when the going gets tough, remember not to be too hard on yourself.

Overcoming Procrastination & Perfectionism

If you have ever put off a task until the last minute or are stressed about completing a task faultlessly, you have likely experienced procrastination and perfectionism. These habits may seem hard to break, but they can be achieved with the right strategies. Although covered in Chapter 4, "Study Smarter, Not Harder," revisiting these concepts from a stress perspective is appropriate.

Break Into Small Manageable Steps

We've all been there before. Faced with a daunting task that feels like a mountain - it may be a lengthy research paper, a complex project, or an impending exam. The enormity of the undertaking can be overwhelming.

However, breaking these tasks into smaller, bite-sized portions can make them more manageable. For instance, given a substantial paper to write, divide it into distinct parts instead of attempting to tackle it all at once. Focus on research in phase one, next on drafting ideas, and last on refining and revising. Each part can also be further subdivided if needed.

Approaching the task one small step at a time makes it less intimidating overall. Moreover, completing each incremental step provides a sense of accomplishment. It is like checking off items on a to-do list; every checkmark added contributes to a feeling of progress and achievement. This positive energy boosts motivation and productivity. Rather than facing an imposing mountain, it is being conquered, one step at a time. Before long, the summit has been reached and the task completed.

Fear Of Failure – It's A Learning Opportunity!

Nobody likes to fail, but the fear of failure can be a formidable barrier that can stop us from even trying. However, everyone makes mistakes - this is perfectly normal! Mistakes offer invaluable lessons that contribute to our learning, growth, and development. Rather than fixating on perfection or the fear of failing, which often results in undue stress and disillusionment, focus on making progress.

Success often comes after numerous setbacks. Michael Jordan, one of the greatest basketball players of all time, once said, "I've missed more than 9,000 shots in my career. I've lost almost 300 games. 26 times, I've been trusted to take the game-winning shot and missed. I've failed over and over and over again in my life. And that is why I succeed."

Mistakes are not failings but opportunities for growth and improvement. It is always beneficial to consider the reasons behind an error. Asking questions like "How could this have been done differently?", "Was more time needed?" or "Was additional help or information required?" can offer clarity. Like in a maze, each wrong turn is not the end but a clue, leading one closer to the destination. Similarly, understanding the reasons behind mistakes serves as guidance, helping to steer towards the correct path. Embrace these moments; they are not setbacks but signposts pointing toward the desired outcome.

Seeing mistakes as opportunities rather than obstacles can shift the fear of failure into a willingness to try and learn. Procrastination and perfectionism, which often go hand-in-hand, do not have to hinder progress and growth. They are just habits that are not set in stone, and with a change in mindset, these behaviors can be reshaped. It takes effort and time. However, each small step to overcome these hurdles improves productivity and lowers stress. With continued effort and practice, breaking free from the cycle of procrastination and the trap of perfectionism is possible.

Building A Positive Mindset

A positive mindset can help you manage stress, overcome challenges, and enjoy life more. This is the power of positive thinking.

Optimism, Gratitude, & Positive Affirmations: Optimism is about looking for the good in situations. When faced with a challenge, try to look for the lessons that can be learned. Reflecting on past challenges successfully handled can help reinforce the understanding that difficulties are transient.

Gratitude centers on valuing what one possesses. A helpful habit is to begin each day by identifying and thinking about what one is thankful for in life.

Positive affirmations such as "I can handle whatever comes my way" or "I'm proud of the progress I'm making" can bolster confidence, aid in stress management, and promote a positive mindset. It is okay to acknowledge hard times but try to maintain perspective and stay optimistic.

Hang Around With Positive People: The company one keeps can significantly shape your mindset. Avoiding those who are pessimistic and spending time with optimistic and supportive individuals, like friends, family, or mentors, offers encouragement and inspiration.

Surround Yourself With Positivity: The surroundings can also influence one's mindset. A happy and welcoming living space, adorned with pictures of loved ones and items that bring joy, contributes to a cheerful atmosphere. Decorating a living area with favorite visuals or creating a comfortable, relaxing space can enhance a positive mindset.

Practicing Mindfulness: This is about being fully present in the moment without judgment. This practice can amplify the enjoyment of good times and promote calmness during challenging periods. Mindfulness can be cultivated through simple practices such as focused breathing, engaging the senses, or meditating each day.

As we close this chapter on mental well-being, remember that college is a time rich with new experiences and opportunities for growth. Embracing this journey involves more than academic achievement; it requires attentiveness to your mental and emotional health. Far from mere buzzwords, they are essential to overall success, affecting study habits, relationships, and pursuing activities you enjoy.

Caring about mental and emotional health is not a sign of weakness but reflects strength, self-awareness, and maturity. When faced with setbacks, view them as temporary and a way to deeper self-understanding. In nurturing your mental and emotional well-being, you're investing in both your collegiate years and in building a brighter, more resilient future.

Chapter 10

How to Thrive on Student Cuisine

" One cannot think well, love well, sleep well,
if one has not dined well."

Virginia Woolf

College is about more than just attending lectures on time and acing exams. They are also about learning to care for your health, starting with what you eat. As the saying goes, "You are what you eat," and we're here to help you achieve vitality, balance, and wellness on a student's budget.

Following on from Chapter 8 on the importance of nutrition for physical health, we continue the discussion in this Chapter by exploring practical ways to achieve healthy eating, including cooking techniques, food safety practices, and budget-friendly meals. We consider the spectrum of available food options, from the on-campus dining hall to the aisles of the local grocery store and even your humble dorm room, equipped with only a microwave and a mini-fridge. We will also discuss how to maintain a balanced diet while coping with the pressures of student life. Eating healthy food that fuels the body and mind is possible without resorting to the stereotypical college diet of instant ramen and vending machine snacks on a daily basis.

For those with access to cooking facilities or a communal kitchen, we will provide tips on food, kitchen safety, meal planning, and how to make your money go further.

Eating healthily while on a budget does not have to mean boring and repetitive meals. With the right strategies, nutritious and delicious food can be enjoyed without overspending. Additionally, we will share some easy, and affordable recipes and food hacks to help kickstart your culinary journey.

By the end of this chapter, you will better understand healthy food options and be more confident in planning and managing your time for healthier eating choices. The lessons learned here will help you survive college and establish good habits for life beyond graduation. After all, taking care of your health is a lifelong investment, and it starts with the food you put on your plate. So, let's dig in!

Campus Cuisine: Diverse Dining Options

One aspect a first-year student encounters is the variety of available food options. Navigating the dining landscape opens a new world of food experiences that cater to various tastes, dietary needs, and schedules. From traditional dining halls offering buffet-style meals to specialty food stations, cafes, and on-campus restaurants, the choice is diverse.

Typically, college dining halls offer a rotating menu that includes everything from comfort food to international cuisine. Vegetarian, vegan, gluten-free, and halal meals are often available for students with dietary restrictions or preferences. Many colleges also host themed food nights or special events that showcase foods from around the world, giving students a taste of different cultures.

Beyond the dining halls, on-campus cafes and restaurants serve a variety of items, such as sandwiches, salads, coffee, baked goods, and more. These spots are great for grabbing a quick bite between classes or for a change of scenery from the dining hall. Additionally, on-campus convenience stores often stock pantry staples, snacks, and ready-to-eat meals for late-night study sessions or quick meals on the go.

The key is balancing enjoying these culinary experiences with healthy and nutritious choices. Here are some suggestions to help guide your food choices and maintain a balanced diet:

Understand Your Meal Plan: Students staying on campus will likely have a meal plan, and it is important to understand how it works. How many meals are included a week? Can meals be used for guests? Are unused meals rolled over to next week, or do they expire? Can meals be used at all dining locations on campus or only certain ones?

Dining Halls: This is the most common option for students. These halls usually offer a diverse range of food stations that serve different types of cuisine and cater to various dietary restrictions. They provide an excellent opportunity to enjoy a balanced meal and a place to catch up with friends.

Cafes & Coffee Shops: These serve coffee, tea, pastries, sandwiches, and sometimes more substantial meals. They are convenient for grabbing a quick bite between classes or when working in a relaxed environment.

On-Campus Restaurants: Some colleges have sit-down restaurants on-site, serving various dishes from casual to gourmet. These are perfect for special occasions or a change from typical cafeteria food.

Food Trucks: Many campuses invite local food trucks to park on-site on specific days, providing diverse, quick, delicious options from different cultures.

Vending Machines: These are usually scattered around campus for a quick drink or snack. While not the best for a full meal, they can provide a quick energy boost.

Campus Convenience Stores: These mini grocery stores stock a range of items from fresh fruits, veggies, and sandwiches to pantry staples, instant meals, and snacks. They are useful for last-minute meal prep or late-night cravings.

Local Restaurants & Takeouts: Explore the local eateries around campus which provide a great way to break from campus food, try new cuisines, and support local businesses. Many places also offer student discounts.

Cooking For Yourself: If a kitchen is available, cooking can be a fun and cost-effective way to eat. By taking charge of ingredients and portions, one can cultivate healthier eating habits and tailor meals to individual tastes. Find local grocery stores to source ingredients for meals.

Meal Kit Delivery Services: Consider subscribing to a meal kit delivery service. These directly deliver pre-portioned ingredients and easy-to-follow recipes to your door, simplifying cooking healthy, diverse meals.

Grocery Delivery Or Pickup Options: These services can be a lifesaver when you cook for yourself but have limited time for regular grocery store visits. You can order precisely what you need, and the items will either be delivered to your door or available for pickup at a convenient time.

But Be Mindful Of The "Freshman 15": This term is often used to describe the weight gain, typically 15 lbs (6.8 kgs), some students may experience during their first year of college. While not a set rule, the combination of stress, irregular schedules, and unlimited dining hall access can lead to unhealthy eating habits. Maintaining a balanced diet and regular exercise routine will help mitigate this risk.

Nutrition & How To Achieve A Balanced Diet

Maintaining a balanced diet is essential for well-being and academic success. It can be challenging to follow healthy eating habits, especially when many tempting, unhealthy food choices exist. However, integrating nutritious foods into daily routines becomes more straightforward with a grasp of healthy eating principles and meal planning.

A balanced diet supports physical health and is crucial for cognitive function, energy levels, and emotional stability. The following sections explore essential aspects of achieving a balanced, nutritious diet for a healthy college life.

Understanding Nutritional Needs: People follow different diets for various reasons, including health, ethics, cultural, or personal preferences. These may include vegetarian, vegan, or gluten-free diets. However, it is possible to maintain balanced nutrition regardless of dietary restrictions. Aim to incorporate foods from various groups, encompassing fruits, vegetables, whole grains, lean proteins, healthy fats, and low-fat dairy products. Additionally, limit salt, added sugars, and trans and saturated fats. This approach guarantees the body receives comprehensive nutrients essential for optimal health.

Don't Skip Breakfast & Avoid Missing Meals! Aim for at least three balanced meals daily, each containing a protein source, a form of carbohydrates, and fruits or vegetables. Start every day with a balanced breakfast to fuel the body and kickstart your metabolism. For sustained energy throughout the day, it is essential to include carbohydrates, proteins, and healthy fats. Examples include oatmeal with nuts and fruits, whole-grain toast with eggs and avocado, or a fruit parfait.

When lacking time for a sit-down meal, grab something healthy on the go, like a banana, a whole-grain bagel, or a yogurt. It is essential not to skip meals, which can lead to overeating later.

Choose Unprocessed Foods: Opt for whole grains, fresh fruits and vegetables, lean proteins, and dairy. Unprocessed foods are generally richer in nutrients.

Limit Processed Foods: While convenient, processed foods typically contain unhealthy levels of fats, salt, and added sugars. Choose fresh food whenever possible.

Limit Added Sugars: Minimize foods and drinks with added sugars, such as sodas, desserts, and candies. These provide many calories but few nutrients.

Control Portions: Use your hand to guide portion sizes: a fist for carbohydrates, a palm for proteins, and a thumb for fats. Aim to fill at least half a plate with fruits or vegetables.

Mindful Eating - Listen To Your Body: Pay attention to what and when you eat. To prevent overeating or when you are emotional, eat only when you are hungry and stop when you are full.

Stay Hydrated: Water is crucial for almost every bodily function. Dehydration can cause fatigue, headaches, and difficulty concentrating. Drink 8 cups or more of fluid daily, preferably water. Limit sugary drinks and caffeine, which can lead to energy crashes. Carry a refillable water bottle and replenish it as required.

Moderate Alcohol Intake: If choosing to drink, always consume alcohol in moderation. Alcohol contains empty calories (i.e. provides little to no nutritional benefit) and may contribute to weight gain.

Smart Snacks: Choose healthy snacks that can provide energy between meals. Fresh fruits, vegetables, nuts, and low-fat yogurt are good choices.

Plan & Prepare: Prepare meals and snacks for the week ahead. This saves time and ensures healthy options are readily available.

It is essential to appreciate that the goal is not perfection but consistent efforts toward balanced, mindful eating. Remember that a balanced diet is not about strict restrictions but more about fueling the body with diverse nutrients, enabling you to function at your best. The habits and knowledge acquired during college help maintain good health and prevent chronic diseases in the future. Your relationship with food is a cornerstone of life, and college is an ideal time to establish a foundation for a future of healthy eating.

Safe Bites: Importance Of Food Hygiene & Safety

This section could quite literally save your life or, at the very least, protect you from food poisoning or a nasty allergic reaction. Prioritizing food hygiene and safety is crucial, particularly in a college environment where eating habits and lifestyles differ significantly from those back home.

Many students will be living independently for the first time, preparing meals, and sharing a communal kitchen. Along with this newfound culinary freedom comes the responsibility of ensuring the food consumed is safe, hygienic, and beneficial to health. Whether a seasoned cook, an amateur, or someone who can just about manage to boil an egg, understanding the basics of food hygiene and safety is crucial.

Food safety is more than keeping utensils clean or cooking meat thoroughly. It is about understanding how diseases can be transmitted through food and how to prevent this from happening. It is about learning to store and prepare food correctly to prevent the growth of harmful bacteria and other pathogens.

This section will cover critical areas, from washing and storing food to safe cooking temperatures and proper handling of leftovers. Awareness of others' dietary restrictions in a communal kitchen can prevent harmful or potentially fatal reactions.

Remember, the goal is not to become a master chef (unless that is your dream!) but to establish safe and hygienic practices. Ultimately, food should be a source of nourishment, pleasure, and communal connection, not a cause for concern or illness.

Wash Hands Thoroughly: Hands can carry many germs. Always wash hands with soap and warm water before handling food and after using the bathroom.

Keep Kitchen Surfaces Clean: Clean countertops, cutting boards and utensils with hot, soapy water. Bacteria can live in many places, and keeping your kitchen clean can prevent them from spreading.

Separate Raw & Cooked Foods: Both raw and cooked foods pose risks of cross-contamination in the kitchen. Raw meat, poultry, and seafood can spread germs to cooked food, leading to foodborne illnesses. To prevent this, separate kitchen utensils should be used to handle raw and cooked foods. Additionally, when handling different raw foods, such as chicken and vegetables, ensure that utensils are thoroughly washed between uses to avoid transferring pathogens.

Store Food Correctly: Different foods require different storage conditions. For example, tomatoes are best stored in a cool, dry place out of direct sunlight, while milk must be refrigerated.

Refrigerate Perishable Food: To prevent bacterial growth, refrigerate leftovers promptly once cooled. Ensure hot foods have cooled to room temperature before storing them in closed containers in the fridge. Aim to refrigerate leftovers within 2 hours of cooking to maintain food safety.

Know Safe Temperatures: Different types of food must be cooked to specific temperatures to kill harmful bacteria. For example, ground meat should be cooked to at least 160°F, poultry to 165°F, and fish to 145°F.

Food Thermometer: Check using a food thermometer to ensure it has been cooked to the correct temperature. Do not rely on color or cooking time alone.

Rinse Fresh Produce: Wash fruits and vegetables under running water before eating or cooking, even if these are to be peeled. This helps remove dirt and contaminants and reduces the risk of foodborne illnesses.

Avoid Eating Raw Or Undercooked Meat: These may contain harmful bacteria, including E. coli and Salmonella. Always cook meat to the recommended temperature.

Understand "Best By" Dates: "Best by" dates are more about quality than safety. Most foods are edible for a limited time after these dates but may not taste as good. Judge the quality by looking at, touching, and smelling the item. Remember, it is better to be safe than sorry, so when in doubt, throw it out.

Avoid Sharing Utensils & Glasses: Sharing such items can spread germs, particularly during flu season. It is advisable to have separate drinking and eating utensils for each individual.

Raw Eggs Danger: Raw eggs can harbor Salmonella bacteria, posing a risk of foodborne illness. This applies to foods such as homemade mayonnaise, ice cream, or cookie dough that contain uncooked eggs.

Be Cautious With Allergens: For individuals with food allergies or friends with allergies, it is **critical** to thoroughly read food labels and inquire about ingredients when dining out.

Thaw Frozen Food Properly: Avoid defrosting food at room temperature, which can promote the growth of harmful pathogens such as Salmonella or E. coli, ultimately leading to food poisoning. Optimal thawing methods include using the refrigerator or microwave or placing the sealed food in cold water.

Avoid Unpasteurized Food & Drinks: Unpasteurized products such as milk, juice, or cheese can contain harmful bacteria. Always choose pasteurized versions.

Be Careful With Buffets: All-you-can-eat buffets can be tempting, especially for students on a tight budget. However, if not correctly maintained, buffets can be a breeding ground for bacteria. Be cautious of food that has not been adequately covered up or looks like it has been sitting out too long.

Symptoms of Food Poisoning: Common signs include upset stomach, fever, vomiting, and diarrhea. If food poisoning is suspected, seeking medical attention promptly is recommended.

Maintain Your Fridge & Freezer: Fridges should be at 40°F (4.4°C) or below, and freezers at 0°F (-17.8°C). These temperature levels help slow the growth of bacteria.

Keep a Well-Stocked & Organized Kitchen: An organized kitchen is a clean kitchen. Having the proper tools and knowing where everything is can help prevent cross-contamination and make food preparation safer.

Safe & Savvy In The Kitchen

A kitchen is filled with potential hazards such as sharp knives, heat sources, electrical appliances, and maybe slippery floors. Each can cause accidents if not handled properly.

This section aims to instill the habit of prioritizing safety in the kitchen. We will cover topics such as proper knife handling, safe appliance usage, fire safety, and how to address minor accidents such as cuts or burns.

Mastering Kitchen Safety

Maintaining safety in the kitchen is not as complicated as it sounds. Simple guidelines and practices can significantly minimize the chance of accidents, ensuring a safe cooking environment.

Understand All Equipment: Each appliance and piece of equipment in a kitchen serves a specific purpose. Be thoroughly familiar with each item's function and safety protocols, including the microwave, toaster, and oven.

Use Appliances Safely: Read the user manual for any new appliances. Do not use them if the cord is frayed or damaged, and never put a fork or other metal object into a plugged-in toaster.

Never Leave Cooking Unattended: This is the number one cause of kitchen fires. If you need to step away, turn off the stove or ask someone to watch the cooking.

Handle Hot Items with Care: When handling hot pots, pans, or baking trays, always use oven mitts for protection. Ensure handles are not protruding from the stove, where they could easily be knocked over. Stay vigilant around hot surfaces, boiling water, and splattering oil or liquids.

Learn Basic First Aid: Knowing how to treat minor cuts or burns can be handy. Keep a first-aid kit accessible in your kitchen or close by.

Keep A Fire Extinguisher: A small kitchen fire can quickly turn into a big one. Having a fire extinguisher nearby and knowing how to use it can prevent a disaster.

Avoid Loose Clothing & Hair: Loose clothing can easily catch fire, and loose hair can fall into the food. If you have long hair, tie it back, and avoid wearing dangling sleeves while cooking.

Clean Spills Immediately: Wet or greasy floors are a slipping hazard. Wipe up all spills on kitchen surfaces or the floor promptly to prevent potential accidents.

Store Heavy Items Properly: Keep heavy pots and pans on lower shelves or in lower cupboards to avoid injury when retrieving or replacing them.

Keep Electrical Appliances Away From Water: These include toasters, mixers, other appliances, and electric sockets. Water and electricity are a dangerous combination.

Ensure Dry Hands When Touching Switches: Hands must be completely dry before touching switches to avoid electric shocks from wet hands.

Keep Kitchen Well-Lit: Good lighting can help prevent accidents. Ensure the kitchen is well-lit to facilitate clear visibility during tasks.

Store Cleaning Products Safely: Keep out of reach of children and away from food storage areas. Many cleaning products are poisonous if ingested.

Dispose Of Broken & Sharp Items Safely: After any breakages, promptly sweep up the pieces and dispose of them properly to lower the risk of injury.

Ensure Appliances are Off: Before leaving the kitchen, make it a habit to check that every appliance, including the oven and stove, has been switched off. This reduces the risk of accidents or fire hazards.

Knife Safety In The Kitchen

Knife safety is of paramount importance as it prevents accidents and potential injuries. Proper knife handling techniques, including keeping a secure grip, using a cutting board, and keeping fingers away from the blade, minimize the risk of slips, cuts, or other mishaps. Additionally, ensuring that knives are sharp and well-maintained enhances control and lowers the likelihood of accidents caused by dull blades. Practicing knife safety creates a safer cooking environment.

Handle With Care: Always hold a knife by its handle and keep your fingers clear of the blade. Even when passing a knife to someone else, offer the handle, not the blade.

Use The Correct Knife For The Task: A small paring knife isn't suitable for chopping large vegetables, just as a bread knife isn't designed for peeling. Using the appropriate knife will help do the cutting job effectively and safely.

Keep Knives Sharp: Dull knives require more pressure to cut, increasing the chance of slipping. Regularly sharpen knives using a sharpening stone or knife sharpener.

Cut Away From The Body: When cutting, slice away from the body and the hand holding the food to prevent potential injuries. Additionally, curl the fingers under when holding food to avoid cuts and accidents.

Secure The Cutting Board: Place a damp cloth or a non-slip mat under the cutting board to prevent it from moving while cutting.

Do Not Leave Knives In The Sink: This can lead to accidental cuts when reaching into the sink. Wash knives immediately after use and store them in a safe place.

Knife Safety In A Dishwasher: Always stack knives with the sharp end pointing downwards in the utensil basket.

Always Pay Attention: Distractions can lead to injuries. Always concentrate on the task when cutting.

Remember, safety in the kitchen is paramount. Follow the above tips to create a safe cooking environment. Safety first, always.

Thrifty Bites: Meal Planning & Healthy Affordable Eating

This section assumes that your student accommodation has a functional kitchen or, at the very least, some basic cooking facilities.

College life is often so busy that it can be challenging to maintain a healthy and balanced diet. Many students resort to fast food, instant ramen, or even skipping meals altogether. To avoid this, plan meals ahead of time.

Helps To Manage Time Better

Planning meals in advance can be a great way to ease the stress of deciding what to eat and reduce the time spent on last-minute grocery runs. By taking a little time to plan ahead, grocery shopping and meal preparation can become more time efficient. This is especially beneficial as students can ensure that they have balanced, nutritious, and easy-to-prepare meals throughout the week. This practice not only saves time but also helps prevent decision fatigue, which can often lead to unhealthy choices when students are too tired or stressed to cook.

Saves Money

Meal planning is a game-changer from a financial standpoint. Students often operate on tight budgets, and frequent eating out or purchasing convenience foods can quickly drain finances. By planning meals, students can make strategic grocery lists, reduce impulse buying, take advantage of sales, and minimize food waste - all of which contribute to substantial savings.

Balanced Nutrition

Meal planning goes beyond the tangible benefits of time and money. It facilitates a healthier lifestyle as you control what you eat. It allows balanced nutrition to be incorporated into the daily routine, thus maintaining energy, focus, and overall health. As such, meal planning becomes a strategy for convenience and a cornerstone of wellness.

Effective Meal Planning

This skill is invaluable and goes beyond merely organizing food; it is about streamlining daily routines, saving resources, and prioritizing health. Meal planning becomes seamless by integrating strategies like theme nights, using meal-planning apps, and cooking in bulk. With meals sorted, students can focus on academics and fully enjoy college.

Remember, a well-fed and nourished student is a happy and productive student!

Start Simple: Choose a day in the week to plan your meals. If you're new to meal planning, start with just a few meals for the week. Starting small prevents feeling overwhelmed, as the focus is only on one week's worth of three meals a day plus snacks. As proficiency grows, gradually expand planning to cover a longer period. Keep a record so that meals can be kept for future use. It can also be expanded upon and improved later as skills improve.

Choose Versatile Ingredients: Ingredients that can be used in multiple recipes will save time and money. For example, chicken can be used in a stir-fry, salad, sandwich, or soup. Similarly, vegetables like bell peppers, broccoli, and spinach can be used in various dishes, including pasta, omelets, and stir-fries.

Invest In Good Storage Containers: A range of quality storage containers is essential for meal prep. Dishes or boxes that are microwave-safe, dishwasher-friendly, and with good seals can make storing, reheating, and transporting meals more manageable.

Create A Grocery Shopping List: Compile a list of all the necessary ingredients for the week according to the meal plan. This practice helps you stay focused during shopping, prevents impulse purchases, and guarantees all essential items are available for cooking.

Utilize A Meal Planning App: Numerous apps are available to help organize recipes, generate shopping lists, and track nutrition. These tools streamline meal planning, enhance efficiency, and can suggest recipes based on pantry ingredients.

Balanced Nutrition: A well-rounded meal plan should encompass all food groups, including protein, carbohydrates, and healthy fats, as well as ample servings of fruits and vegetables. This approach guarantees balanced and fulfilling meals that provide essential nutrients for optimal bodily function.

Easy Breakfasts: This is often the meal students skip the most. Opt for easy breakfast options such as overnight oats or yogurt with granola and fruit that can be prepared the night before.

Remember Snacks & Hydration: Incorporate healthy snack options into your plan, such as cut-up vegetables, fruits, yogurt, or nuts, to sustain energy between meals and deter unhealthy snacking. Additionally, ensure easy access to hydration by utilizing a reusable water bottle nearby to stay adequately hydrated throughout the day.

Try Themed Meal Days: Incorporating themed meals can make planning fun and add variety. Consider designating specific days for themes like Meatless Mondays, Taco Tuesdays, or Slow Cooker Sundays. This approach can streamline recipe selection and add creativity to meal planning, making it more engaging and enjoyable.

Make Use Of Convenient Products: While fresh is best, remember frozen or canned vegetables, fruits, and proteins. These can be lifesavers when you are short on time, or fresh produce is out of season. Canned food can be just as nutritious, but check labels for added sugars, sodium, or preservatives. With a bit of attention to detail, you can find high-quality options that suit your dietary needs.

Schedule Time To Prep: Set aside a specific time each week to plan, shop, and prepare meals. This might be a few hours on a weekend day or an hour each night. Consistency is key; making meal planning and preparation a routine will help it become a sustainable habit.

Cook With Friends: Transform meal prepping into a social gathering to enhance enjoyment and distribute the workload. Collaborating with friends makes the process more enjoyable, facilitates sharing meal ideas, and enables learning from each other's cooking techniques.

Maintain A Stocked Pantry: Storing staples such as rice, pasta, canned vegetables, herbs and spices, oils, and vinegar facilitates meal preparation when planning time is limited or when the refrigerator is running low on ingredients.

Stay Organized: Centralize all recipes, shopping lists, and meal plans in one location, whether a notebook, an online document, or a digital app. This approach simplifies access to past plans and favorite recipes, aiding in recalling meals that were most successful for your needs.

Experiment & Explore: Be bold and try new recipes or ingredients. Variety is the spice of life and keeps meal planning and eating exciting. If a recipe doesn't work out, consider it a learning experience – discovering your taste preferences is also part of the process!

Be Flexible: Your meal plan is not set in stone but adaptable. Life happens, and unexpected events may arise, such as cravings for something different or invitations to dine out. Planning meals aims to make your life easier and healthier, not to create stress, so it is important to allow for flexibility.

Affordable Eating For Students

At college, juggling numerous responsibilities is likely part of the daily routine, and managing finances is no exception. While expenses like tuition, books, and housing are often non-negotiable, the food budget is one area where considerable control can be exerted. Learning to save money on meals is not only a short-term necessity but also a valuable skill that will serve you well beyond graduation.

Eating well without breaking the bank is possible with thoughtful planning and mindful shopping. Below are some strategies to help save money while still eating well:

Do Your Own Cooking: This is the best way to save money. Home-cooked meals are cheaper and often healthier than eating out or ordering in. Ideally, learn basic cooking skills and gather a few favorite recipes before heading to college. However, even if you're already in college, there is always time to start cooking your own meals and saving money.

Meal Prep In Bulk: Prepare larger quantities of a dish, dividing them into individual portions to last for multiple meals. This method saves time on busy days when cooking is not feasible. For example, a large batch of chili or stew can provide several meals that can be frozen and reheated as required. However, it is essential to be mindful of available food storage space, especially when sharing with other students.

Leftover Magic: Plan to use excess food creatively to reduce waste and maximize cooking efforts. For example, leftover chicken can be added to a salad or wrap, or leftover vegetables can be tossed into an omelet or soup.

Meal Planning & Prep: Planning and preparing meals in advance often saves money on food costs. It enables purchases and cooking in bulk, takes advantage of special offers, and decreases impulse buying and food waste.

Buy Non-Perishables In Bulk: Items such as rice, pasta, dried beans, canned goods, and frozen fruits and veggies can be bought in bulk, especially when on sale. These items last longer and can be used in various meals, saving money over time.

Eat Less Meat: Meat is usually one of the most expensive items when shopping for food. Instead, incorporate more plant-based proteins into meals, like lentils, beans, tofu, or chickpeas. These are nutritious, filling, and often cheaper. Perhaps start with a Meatless Monday and see how it goes.

Bring Own Snacks & Drinks: Buying snacks or coffee on campus can quickly add up. Instead, bring homemade snacks, water, and coffee or tea. This approach helps save money and enables healthier choices.

Use Student Discounts: Many grocery stores and restaurants offer student discounts. Don't be shy about asking or signing up for these; they can lead to considerable savings over time.

Eating Out & Ordering In: Try to limit takeouts and restaurant dining to occasional treats rather than the norm. These options are considerably more expensive and can rapidly deplete your food budget and overall finances.

Seasonal Produce: In-season fruits and vegetables are usually cheaper and fresher. Farmers markets can be an excellent source for these deals.

Do Not Shop When Hungry! Ensure a full stomach before shopping. An empty stomach significantly increases the likelihood of making impulsive and unhealthy purchases.

Share Costs With Roommates: Sharing the cost of everyday items or cooking is a great way to reduce expenses and enjoy meals together.

Finding Inspiration: Easy Recipe Ideas

Numerous resources are available where college students can find easy, cheap, and healthy recipe ideas. Here are a few:

Websites & Blogs: Many specialize in budget-friendly and easy-to-follow recipes. There is a treasure trove of diverse and creative recipes that cater to different taste buds, dietary preferences, cooking experience levels, and budgets. Whether it is an easy, quick, dorm-friendly meal, a nutritious budget-friendly option, or a gourmet experiment, websites and blogs offer a vast menu of culinary possibilities.

Cooking Apps: Numerous digital apps offer a diverse range of recipes, along with details such as cost per serving, total prep and cook time, and user reviews, to help students decide what to prepare. Recipe apps have become a popular source of culinary inspiration for many students, offering convenience with features like ingredient-based recipe searches or barcode scanning at the grocery store. With step-by-step instructions and handy cooking timers, these apps provide valuable kitchen assistance, empowering students to become confident and creative home chefs.

Social Media: Platforms like TikTok, Instagram, and Pinterest can be goldmines for recipe ideas. YouTube's instructive recipe videos help provide a visual step-by-step guide to cooking. With countless food influencers and passionate home cooks, there is plenty of inspiration geared toward student budgets and tastes. Search for relevant hashtags like #cheapmeals or #collegerecipes.

Cookbooks: Many focus specifically on students and budget cooking. These books offer concise step-by-step instructions and straightforward recipes with affordable ingredients, making it easier to prepare tasty meals without breaking the bank. Search online, on Amazon, or visit bookstores for the most popular titles or those that meet your requirements and tastes.

University Resources: Some colleges provide websites or cooking classes to help students with limited funding learn to cook and eat healthily.

Food Banks & Community Centers: These places sometimes offer free cooking classes or budget-friendly recipe ideas.

Friends & Family: Don't forget about your network. Parents, grandparents, older siblings (especially those who have been to college), and friends can be a wealth of knowledge on easy and affordable meals.

Inspire Yourself: Experimenting can be an inspiration in itself! Exploring new recipes and ingredients in the kitchen can inspire creativity and excitement in meal preparation and offer valuable learning opportunities.

Creating tasty and nutritious meals on a student's budget can be simple and inexpensive if you have the right resources.

99 Food Hacks Every Student Should Know

Below are some food hacks designed to streamline the culinary journey, making it easier, quicker, and more enjoyable while maintaining taste and nutritional value. These hacks simplify the cooking process, save precious time, and optimize the longevity and flavor of food. From innovative uses of common kitchen appliances and storage techniques to efficient cooking methods, below offers a collection of easy food hacks and practical, time-saving tips tailored for busy college students. While these food hacks aim to enhance your culinary experience, individual results may vary. Always exercise caution and follow proper food safety practices when trying new techniques or recipes.

1. **Microwave More:** Use the microwave to cook pasta, rice, and scrambled eggs. Do some research on microwave cooking to expand your options.

2. **Upgrade Instant Ramen:** Add vegetables, protein (like eggs or tofu), and spices to instant ramen for a more balanced meal.

3. **Frozen Veggie Boost**: Always have frozen vegetables on hand; they are just as nutritious as fresh ones, last longer, and can be used right out of the freezer. Toss into stir-fries, pasta, or microwaved meals for added nutrition.

4. **Frozen Fruit Smoothie Packs:** Pre-pack smoothie ingredients in Ziplock bags. Freeze them and add milk or juice into a blender when needed.

5. **Spice It Up:** Keep a variety of spices on hand to quickly add flavor to meals without adding extra calories or salt.

6. **Freeze Sliced Bread:** If unable to finish a loaf of bread before it goes stale, store it in the freezer and toast slices without defrosting beforehand as needed.

7. **Master the Art of Sandwiches:** With endless combinations of bread, proteins, cheeses, veggies, and spreads, sandwiches can be quick, easy, and nutritious.

8. **Hard-Boiled Eggs:** Make a batch of these for quick, protein-rich snacks or to add to meals.

9. **1 Minute Cookie in a Mug:** Mix a small amount of butter, brown sugar, flour, an egg yolk, and chocolate chips in a microwave-safe mug; microwave for about 60 seconds for a quick cookie treat.

10. **Mug Desserts**: Master a few microwave mug dessert recipes for those late-night cravings. Brownies and cakes, for example, can all be made.

11. **Banana Ice Cream Substitute:** Blend frozen bananas to make a dairy-free, healthy ice cream alternative.

12. **Oven-to-Toastie Hack:** Don't have a sandwich press? Make a toastie in the oven by wrapping a sandwich in foil and placing it under a heated oven-safe dish.

13. **Use an Iron to Make Grilled Cheese:** A grilled cheese sandwich can be made with an iron and aluminum foil. Afterward, clean the iron, and don't use steam.

14. **Greek Yogurt Everything:** This can be a healthy substitute for sour cream, mayonnaise, and cream cheese in many recipes.

15. **Quick Omelets in a Mug:** Crack eggs into a microwave-safe mug, add other ingredients such as chopped veggies, cheese, and ham or bacon, stir, and cover. Depending on the wattage of the microwave, cook for 1-2 minutes. Instant omelet!

16. **Spice Up Popcorn:** Add spices like cinnamon, chili powder, or nutritional yeast to popcorn for a healthy snack with a flavor boost.

17. **Roll Citrus:** Roll lemons or limes on the counter before cutting to get more juice out.

18. **Avocado Ripening:** Speed up the ripening process by storing avocados in a paper bag with a banana.

19. **Bowl Hack:** Don't have a plate? Use a wide, shallow bowl instead.

20. **Peel Ginger with a Spoon:** It is easier and wastes less than using a knife.

21. **Preserve Herbs**: Freeze fresh herbs in ice cube trays with olive oil or water to preserve them for later use in cooking.

22. **Want to Cool a Beverage Quickly?** Wrap a wet paper towel around the can or bottle and place it in the freezer for about 15 minutes.

23. **Ripe Pineapple:** Pull on the leaves of a pineapple to test ripeness. If they come out easily, it's ripe.

24. **Fruit Salad Storage:** Store fruit salad in a mason jar to keep it fresh longer.

25. **Use a Pizza Cutter:** These cutters can be used for more than just pizza. They can also cut sandwiches, pancakes, waffles, frozen herbs, and more.

26. **Canned Goods:** Keep a stock of canned goods like beans, tuna, and tomatoes. They're affordable, long-lasting, and can be used in many meals.

27. **Check Egg Freshness:** Place the egg in a bowl of water. If it floats, it's old. If it sinks, it's fresh.

28. **DIY Latte:** Make a latte by shaking hot milk and instant coffee in a sealed jar.

29. **Breakfast Burrito in a Mug:** Layer tortilla pieces, scrambled eggs, cheese, and salsa in a microwave-safe mug. Microwave until heated through, then enjoy a convenient breakfast on the go.

30. **Slow Potato Sprouting:** Store apples and potatoes together to

prevent the potatoes from growing.

31. **Revive Stale Bread:** Wet stale (but not moldy) bread with water, then bake at 350°F for a few minutes until crispy.

32. **Peel Kiwi with a Spoon**: Cut the top off a kiwi and then scoop out the fruit with a spoon.

33. **Less Mess Cheese Grating:** Freeze cheese for 15 minutes before grating.

34. **Coffee Ice Cubes:** Don't waste leftover coffee - freeze in an ice cube tray and use later in iced coffee. This will prevent the drink from getting diluted as the ice cube melts.

35. **Veggie Chips:** For a healthy snack option, turn leftover vegetables like kale, zucchini, or sweet potatoes into crispy chips. Slice thinly, toss with olive oil and seasonings, and bake until crispy.

36. **Instant Iced Coffee:** Brew a strong cup of coffee, then pour it over a glass of ice.

37. **DIY Microwave Popcorn:** Use regular popcorn kernels and a paper bag. It's cheaper and healthier.

38. **Easy Peel Garlic**: Put garlic cloves in a jar, shake vigorously, and the peel will come right off. Alternatively, microwave a garlic bulb for 20 seconds to make the cloves easier to peel.

39. **Revive Wilted Veggies:** Soak wilted vegetables in ice water for about 15 minutes to revive them.

40. **Fruit-Infused Water:** For a refreshing drink, fill a bottle halfway with lemon slices and frozen berries, then fill the rest with water. Experiment with other fruits and herbs.

41. **No Time to Cook?** Think cheese, crackers, fruit, and raw veggies.

42. **Easy-Open Bananas:** Open bananas from the bottom - it's easier and prevents squishing.

43. **Pancake Mix in a Ketchup Bottle:** Store pancake batter in a clean squeezy bottle for easy and mess-free pancake making.

44. **Coffee Filter Snack Bowl:** A coffee filter makes a perfect makeshift

snack bowl for popcorn or chips.

45. **Cook Pasta in a Coffee Maker or Kettle**: In the absence of a stove, pasta can be boiled in a coffee maker or kettle. Ensure this is clean and free of limescale beforehand.

46. **Save the Avocado:** Store cut avocados with a chunk of onion in an airtight container to prevent browning.

47. **Avocado as Butter:** Swap butter for avocado on toast for a healthier alternative.

48. **Quick Ripen Bananas**: Bake unripe bananas unpeeled at 300°F in the oven for about an hour.

49. **Fruit as Ice Cubes:** Freeze grapes or berries and use them as flavorful, edible ice cubes in drinks.

50. **Ice Cream Scoop Hack:** Warm your ice cream scoop under hot water for easier scooping.

51. **Freeze Leftover Soup in a Muffin Tin:** Then transfer portions to a freezable food bag for individual servings.

52. **Easy Microwave Cleaning:** Heat a bowl of vinegar and water in the microwave, then wipe it clean. The steam will loosen any food stuck on the walls.

53. **Smart Storage for Bananas**: Separate bananas from the bunch and wrap the stems in plastic wrap to keep them fresher for longer.

54. **Use a Hot Glass to Soften Butter:** Warm up a glass by running it under hot water or microwaving it for a few seconds, then cover over the butter to soften it quickly.

55. **Toaster Bags for Grilled Cheese:** If without a stove, toaster bags are a neat trick for making grilled cheese in a pop-up toaster.

56. **Measuring Sticky Ingredients:** Spray a measuring cup with cooking spray before measuring items like honey or peanut butter to prevent them from sticking.

57. **Quick Oven Baked Potatoes:** Speed up the cooking time of a potato in an oven by pushing a metal skewer through it before baking. The metal will conduct heat and cook the potato from the inside out.

58. **Oven Tortilla Chips:** Cut tortillas into triangles, spray with oil, add a little salt, then bake in the oven for quick DIY chips.

59. **DIY Steam Bags:** Add vegetables and a tablespoon of water to a microwaveable zip-top bag. Seal the bag and pierce holes in it to allow steam to escape. Microwave on high for 2-3 minutes or until the vegetables are tender.

60. **Easiest Peel Boiled Eggs:** Add a teaspoon of baking soda to water when boiling eggs to make them easier to peel.

61. **Keep Salad Greens Fresh:** Put a paper towel in a salad greens container to absorb excess moisture and keep them fresher for longer.

62. **Freeze Wine:** Freeze leftover wine in ice cube trays to use in future cooking recipes.

63. **Grate Cold Butter:** To make butter spreading easier or to use in recipes, use a cheese grater to shred the cold butter into small pieces.

64. **DIY Popsicles:** Freeze fruit juice, yogurt, or smoothies in an ice cube tray with toothpicks or popsicle sticks for a quick, refreshing snack.

65. **Easy Clean Blender:** To clean a blender, fill it 50% with warm water, add a few drops of dish soap, blend for a few seconds, and then rinse.

66. **Extend Ice Cream Shelf Life:** Place plastic wrap on the ice cream before replacing the lid to prevent ice crystals.

67. **Ripen Fruit Fast:** Put unripe fruit in a bag with a banana to ripen it faster. Bananas release ethylene, a natural gas that speeds up the ripening process.

68. **Instant Oats**: These are quick and easy to prepare for a healthy breakfast or snack.

69. **Silicone Muffin Cups**: They are perfect for making individual portions of muffins, egg bakes, or mini-meals.

70. **Cook Extra Protein**: Cook extra chicken, tofu, or other proteins for salads, wraps, or other meals throughout the week.

71. **Mason Jar Salads**: Layer salad ingredients in a mason jar for a grab-and-go meal. Put heavier ingredients at the bottom with

lettuce at the top to prevent sogginess.

72. **Use Every Bit of Nutella**: When your Nutella jar is almost empty, fill it with ice cream to get the last delicious bits out.

73. **Make Instant Frothy Drink:** Shake dairy or non-dairy milk in a microwaveable jar and then microwave for instant frothy milk for coffee or hot chocolate.

74. **Iced Tea**: Brew tea in a coffee maker for a quick batch of iced tea. Chill and serve.

75. **Fast Freezer Sandwiches**: Prep several sandwiches and wrap each in foil. Freeze them so they are ready for quick grilling, toasting or microwaving.

76. **Pita Pizza**: Use pita bread as a quick pizza base. Top with sauce, cheese, and toppings, then bake or microwave.

77. **Yogurt Parfait in a Mug:** Layer yogurt, granola, and fresh fruit in a mug for a quick and customizable breakfast option. Repeat layers as desired, then enjoy a nutritious and satisfying morning meal.

78. **Easy Quesadillas**: Place cheese and fillings between two tortillas, wrap in aluminum foil, then iron for a quick quesadilla.

79. **Cereal Snack Mix**: Combine cereal, nuts, dried fruits, and chocolate chips for a custom snack.

80. **Mini Fridge Freezer Magic**: Turn your mini fridge's freezer into a makeshift ice cream maker. Mix ingredients in a bag, freeze, and knead occasionally.

81. **2-Minute French Toast**: Soak bread in a mix of egg, milk, and cinnamon, then microwave in a mug or container for quick French toast.

82. **Toothpick Sandwich Holder**: Use toothpicks to keep wraps or sandwiches from unraveling.

83. **Quick Steam Veggies**: Place veggies in a microwave-safe bowl, add water, cover with a plate, and microwave to steam.

84. **Spice It Up**: Create a mini spice kit with your favorite seasonings to elevate any dorm-made dish. Or fill an empty Tic Tac box with

preferred spices as a flavor enhancer for on-the-go meals.

85. **DIY Snack Bars**: Combine oats, honey, dried fruits, and nuts. Press into a pan, chill, and cut for homemade snack bars.
86. **Hack Instant Oatmeal**: Mix peanut butter, fresh fruits, or chocolate chips for a flavor-packed breakfast.
87. **Portable Pancakes**: Make a big batch of pancakes and freeze. Reheat later in the microwave directly from the freezer for a quick breakfast.
88. **Canned Tuna Twist**: Enhance canned tuna with mayo, lemon juice, and spices. Use it as a sandwich spread or salad topping.
89. **Bagel Sandwich**: Use as a sandwich base. Bagels are filling and an alternative to regular bread.
90. **DIY Frozen Burritos**: Make burritos in bulk, wrap them in foil, and freeze them. Remove the foil and microwave when hungry.
91. **DIY Hummus**: Blend canned chickpeas into hummus with olive oil, garlic, and lemon juice.
92. **Flavor Boost with Broth**: Cook grains like rice or quinoa in chicken or vegetable stock for added taste.
93. **Microwave Lemons**: Microwave lemons for 10 seconds before squeezing to extract more juice.
94. **Quick Dessert Wrap**: Spread peanut butter and sliced bananas on a tortilla, roll it up, and microwave for a sweet treat. Experiment with other favorite ingredients.
95. **Potato Chip Crunch**: Crush leftover chips and use them as a crispy topping for salads or casseroles.
96. **Fridge Deodorizer**: Place a bowl of baking soda in the fridge to absorb odors.
97. **Soda Pop Chicken**: Marinate chicken in cola or root beer to tenderize and add flavor.
98. **Crispy Microwave Bacon**: Lay bacon strips on an upside-down bowl with a plate underneath in the microwave to allow excess grease to drain and achieve crispier results.

99. **Easy Mac 'n Cheese:** Mix cooked pasta, shredded cheese, and a splash of milk in a microwave-safe bowl. Microwave until creamy and well combined.

Remember that dining at college is more than just grabbing a quick bite between classes. It's about learning to nourish your body and mind with balanced meals, even on a tight student budget. In this chapter, we've navigated the on-campus dining options, discovered how to maintain a balanced diet amidst the hectic college schedule, and shared practical tips for cooking in limited kitchen spaces. We've also covered the importance of food safety, budget-friendly shopping, and how to enjoy diverse and nutritious meals without falling into the monotonous trap of instant ramen.

From the dining hall to your dorm room, you're now equipped with strategies to eat well and make every meal count. By applying these principles, you are setting yourself up for a healthier lifestyle that will benefit you throughout your college years and beyond. So, take this knowledge, get creative in the kitchen, and embrace the joy of cooking and eating well at college!

Chapter II

Money Management For Students

" You must gain control over your money or the lack of it will forever control you. "

Dave Ramsey

With greater independence comes the important responsibility of looking after your money. For many students, this may be the first time that they are responsible for managing their finances, from basic budgeting to addressing more complex matters such as investing and handling student loans. While the primary focus is on academic and personal development, cultivating good financial habits is also essential, as they will serve as a concrete foundation for future financial health.

Money management is not only about paying bills on time or avoiding debt, though these are important aspects. It is also about understanding the value of money, making informed decisions about spending and saving, setting and working towards financial goals, and learning how to navigate the economic landscape. It is about realizing that every financial decision made today can impact life after graduation.

This chapter aims to help you manage your finances effectively during college. It will explore budgeting, saving, credit, debt, and the significance of financial education. Additionally, it will discuss living within your means, the value of part-time work or internships, planning for the future and avoiding impulsive spending.

Mastering all these aspects will facilitate financial stability and freedom, i.e., the ability to make choices in life without being excessively burdened by financial constraints. With knowledge and practice, you will begin to see money not as a source of stress but as a tool that, when used wisely, can open doors to opportunities and a secure future.

Remember that learning to manage finances is a step-by-step process. You are not expected to be an expert right away; everyone makes mistakes. The key is to learn from these mistakes, continue to educate yourself and take steps towards better financial habits. Financial health is an integral part of overall well-being, and it is never too early to start cultivating a positive and proactive approach to managing your finances.

Disclaimer: The financial advice provided is for general informational purposes only and should not be considered professional financial advice. Before making any significant financial decisions, it is essential to conduct thorough research and consult with a qualified financial advisor. Additionally, individual financial situations may vary, so the strategies outlined here may not be suitable for everyone.

The Money Pit: Top Student Mistakes

College can be challenging for newly independent students when managing their own money, especially when this is for the first time. Unfortunately, many make common mistakes due to not understanding the complexities of the financial world. It is, therefore, crucial to be aware of these dangers and take proactive measures to prevent them from happening. Below are some of the mistakes commonly made:

Not Following A Budget: Many students fail to create or follow a budget, which can lead to overspending and financial stress. Without a budget, it can be difficult to keep track of income and expenses and understand where money has gone.

Overspending On Credit Cards: While helpful, credit cards can lead to significant debt if not used responsibly. Students sometimes fall into the trap of spending beyond their means because they can easily access funds.

Poor Saving Habits: Some fail to save any money before or during college, leaving them unprepared for unexpected expenses or financial emergencies. Saving even a small amount regularly can make a difference over time.

Peer Pressure: Your friends might not be in the same financial situation or have your spending habits. It is okay to say no to expensive outings or purchases that do not align with your budget. Remember, it is your money and your financial future at stake.

Impulse Spending: College provides many opportunities for expenditure; impulse buying can quickly deplete a student's budget and lead to financial difficulties.

Not Taking Advantage Of Student Discounts: Many discounts are available to students, and ignoring or not finding out about these can result in unnecessary spending.

Misunderstanding Student Loans: Not fully appreciating the terms of such loans, including interest rates and repayment plans, can lead to financial strain after graduation. Borrowing only what is needed and having a repayment plan is crucial.

Ignoring Financial Aid Opportunities: Many students are not aware of all the options available, including scholarships, grants, and work-study programs. Missing out on these opportunities can mean taking on more debt than is absolutely necessary.

Not Planning For Emergencies: Not having an emergency fund can leave students vulnerable to unexpected costs, such as computer repairs or medical bills. This can lead to unnecessary stress or even more debt if borrowing is needed to cover these expenses.

Not Being Thrifty: Some students overlook simple, frugal practices, like cooking themselves instead of eating out, using public transport instead of owning a car or buying used textbooks instead of new versions. Being thrifty does not mean living without enjoyment or convenience; it is just about making thoughtful decisions about spending and finding cost-effective alternatives. Every little bit saved helps!

Not Living Within Your Means: Don't try to keep up with the Joneses! It is common for students to spend money on unnecessary expenses or engage in activities they are not genuinely interested in just to fit in or feel accepted. Be mindful of your financial limitations and prioritize your needs over your wants. Only spend on what you can afford!

Eating Out Too Often: While convenient, eating out regularly can quickly drain the bank account. Consider cooking at home and packing lunches to save money. If you go out, opt for special deals or happy hours to get the most bang for your buck.

Not Monitoring Your Bank Account: Regularly checking the bank balance can help identify mistakes, avoid overdraft fees, and stay aware of your financial position.

Failing To Protect Personal Information: Identity theft can lead to severe financial harm. Students must be careful about sharing personal information, especially online, and regularly check their credit reports for any signs of suspicious activity.

These pitfalls often faced by students can be minimized through early education and preparation. Use resources such as books, blogs, podcasts, and online courses. Talk to friends and family to gain an appreciation for topics like debt, budgeting, and spending. Financial literacy is a valuable life skill that will benefit you long after graduation.

Budgeting: The Heart Of Sound Financial Management

At the core of financial management lies the concept of budgeting, which enables individuals to understand their financial position better. Budgeting involves creating a plan - a budget - to allocate and manage money effectively.

For a student, budgeting can ensure funds are allocated for essential items and meaningful activities. Whether relying on savings, parental support, scholarships, or part-time employment, having clarity on expenditure instills a sense of financial control and peace of mind.

How To Budget

Identify Income / Funds: Your money coming in may include financial aid, money from part-time jobs, internships, money from parents, savings, etc. When considering income, it is best to count only net income (i.e. the money remaining after any taxes).

List Expenses: Identify where money is spent each month. Start with fixed expenses, such as tuition, rent, or monthly subscriptions. Next, look at variable costs such as groceries, eating out, transport, personal care, entertainment, etc. Do not forget occasional costs like books, travel, or gifts.

Compare Income vs Expenses: This is where the reality check happens. If income is higher than expenses, you are in a good position! The extra money can be used to pay off debt faster, save, or invest. However, if expenses exceed income, some changes must be made.

Make Adjustments: Look for non-essential items to cut back on. This may include dining out, entertainment, clothes, or unnecessary subscriptions. Remember, it is essential to live within your means.

Save For Future Goals: If money remains after covering expenses, allocate some of it to savings, whether for travel, an emergency fund, or future investments.

Budgeting Spreadsheet: Utilize Excel or Google Sheets to construct a budget tailored to your specific requirements. To help you get started, we have enclosed below a sample budget template that comprises essential considerations for your budgeting process.

Student Budgeting Template

Download a customizable version of this spreadsheet at https://bit.ly/uni-college-guide

FIXED EXPENSES:	DAILY	WEEKLY	MONTHLY	SEMESTER	ANNUAL	NOTES
Rental / Housing						
Food / Meal Plan						
Tuition & Fees						
Loan / Credit Cards						
Cell Phone						
Utilities						
Car						
Insurance						
Add Entry...						
TOTAL FIXED EXPENSES	$ -	$ -	$ -	$ -	$ -	
FLEXIBLE EXPENSES:	DAILY	WEEKLY	MONTHLY	SEMESTER	ANNUAL	NOTES
Books						
Clothes						
Entertainment/Recreation						
Eating Out						
Travel/Transport						
Internet						
Toiletries						
Gym/Sports						
Laundry						
Savings						
Add Entry...						
TOTAL FLEXIBLE EXPENSES	$ -	$ -	$ -	$ -	$ -	
SOURCES OF INCOME:	DAILY	WEEKLY	MONTHLY	SEMESTER	ANNUAL	NOTES
Financial Aid/Student Loans						
Jobs (after taxes)						
Parents/Family						
Investments/Savings						
Add Entry...						
TOTAL INCOME	$ -	$ -	$ -	$ -	$ -	
SUMMARY	DAILY	WEEKLY	MONTHLY	SEMESTER	YEARLY	NOTES
Total Income:	$ -	$ -	$ -	$ -	$ -	
Total Fixed Expenses:	$ -	$ -	$ -	$ -	$ -	
Total Flexible Expenses:	$ -	$ -	$ -	$ -	$ -	
DIFFERENCE:	$ -	$ -	$ -	$ -	$ -	

Disclaimer: This spreadsheet is designed to aid students in managing finances and includes common income and expense categories. It may not encompass all possible financial scenarios, so users should tailor it to fit their personal needs and seek professional advice as necessary. The creators are not liable for financial outcomes or errors resulting from the use of this template. This tool is for guidance only and not intended for use as the exclusive basis for financial decisions.

To enable editing and tailoring to your specific needs, a customizable version of this spreadsheet is available to download from https://bit.ly/uni-college-guide (or scan the QR code towards the back of the book.). Basic formulas have been included to automate the main calculations. Please ensure these formulas stay accurate if assumptions or conditions change or new rows or columns are added or deleted.

Review & Adjust Regularly: A budget is not a set-and-forget tool. It should be reviewed regularly and adjusted as necessary. Income and expenses can change over time, and your budget needs to reflect these changes.

Digital Tools Can Make Budgeting Easier: Many free and paid apps can track income and expenses, categorize spending, set spending limits for each category, and even send alerts when nearing such limits. Apps can also simplify the budgeting process and provide convenient access to financial information anywhere via a cellphone.

Should A Budget Be Set Weekly Or Monthly?

The frequency chosen to review a budget largely depends on individual circumstances, income schedules, and spending habits. Some prefer to budget weekly, while others favor monthly, quarterly, or longer. Let's take a closer look at both weekly and monthly budgeting:

Weekly Budgeting: This can be useful for those who are paid weekly or new to budgeting. There may be comparatively fewer entries, so it is simpler to track smaller amounts of money movements over a shorter period. This method provides a more immediate overview of finances and can help highlight impulsive or excessive spending faster.

However, weekly budgeting may make planning for larger, less frequent expenses, such as monthly rent or tuition fees, more challenging. It also requires greater time commitment since it needs to be updated more frequently.

Monthly Budgeting: This is a standard frequency, particularly for those who are paid monthly or have significant monthly financial obligations such as rent. It allows a broader view of income and expenses and may be more convenient to match the budgeting frequency with when bills are due.

A monthly budget makes planning for more significant expenses and irregular bills easier. However, it might lead to overspending early in the month and, therefore, a shortfall later. Maintaining discipline in tracking spending throughout the month is crucial. Good record-keeping becomes especially important to ensure all expenses are accounted for, especially given the potential delay of 3 or 4 weeks from the spending date.

In the end, there is no one-size-fits-all answer. Some may even find that a combination of the two works best. For example, a broad monthly budget could handle recurring, fixed costs. Then, a weekly budget can be used for discretionary spending, including eating out, entertainment, and personal care items. Regardless of the chosen method, selecting a system that works for you is vital. The goal is to understand the sources of income and expenditure, enabling smarter financial decision-making.

Remember, a budget is not designed to limit freedom but to enhance it. It facilitates control over money and lowers the chance of overspending. Although it may be challenging to maintain this initially, budgeting can reduce money worries and contribute to a healthier financial future once it becomes a habit.

How To Track Spending

When it comes to managing money, awareness is power. One of the best ways to be fully aware is by tracking your spending. It is an essential practice that goes hand in hand with successful budgeting. Remember, tracking spending is not a punishment but a tool to understand financial habits. It allows for the awareness of how funds have been spent - whether towards essentials like rent and groceries or discretionary expenses such as dining out and entertainment.

By gaining this insight, distinctions can be made between needs and wants, patterns and potential pitfalls in spending habits can be identified, and informed decisions can be made that align with financial goals. Understanding spending habits enables the identification of areas of potential overspending and finding ways to cut back and save.

Monitoring expenditure is a proactive approach that encourages responsibility and nurtures a sense of control over finances. Remember, the path to financial wellness begins with being fully aware of expenses. Here are some steps to effectively track spending:

Choose Your Method: There are several ways to track spending, including traditional methods such as recording expenses in a notebook, keeping receipts, or using a spreadsheet. Alternatively, use a personal finance app or software to automate the process and categorize spending.

Record Every Purchase: No matter how small the amount, note down every purchase made. The little, frequent purchases often add up and can throw a budget off balance. Include everything from rent and bills to coffee and snacks.

Categorize Expenses: Group expenditures into categories such as rent, groceries, utilities, transportation, entertainment, etc. This will provide a clearer picture of where most of the money goes. Most budgeting apps will automatically do this.

Set A Time To Review: Regularly review recorded expenses. This could be daily, weekly, or monthly, depending on what is the most convenient. Look for patterns and areas of potential overspending.

Automate The Process: Consider using a budgeting app or software that can link to bank accounts and credit cards. These tools can automatically track and categorize spending, and many offer alerts if spending nears budget limits in any category.

Stay Consistent: Consistency is vital to successfully tracking expenditures. Make it a part of a routine, and it will provide ongoing insights into financial habits.

Decoding Your Financial Aid Package

The financial aid package is a lifeline for many students making a college education possible. It is a complex mosaic of various sources of funds, including scholarships, grants, work-study opportunities, and loans.

It is critical to understand the components of your financial aid package, including distinguishing between free money (e.g. scholarships and grants) and borrowed money (e.g. federal and private loans). It is also essential to appreciate the long-term implications of accepting this aid. You must also understand the fine print, the terms and conditions, the repayment schedules, and the interest rates associated with the aid.

With a clear grasp of all these aspects, planning spending, calculating post-graduation debt, and discovering opportunities to reduce reliance on loans become feasible. It aids in planning a future with less debt and more financial freedom. So, let's unravel the often confusing but essential world of financial aid packages.

Common Types of Financial Aid

Understanding the financial aid package is essential to making informed decisions about which components to accept, recognizing the long-term implications of these choices, and creating a plan to cover any remaining costs effectively. This step is crucial in managing college finances and minimizing debt upon graduation.

Grants & Scholarships: These originate from various sources, such as the federal government, your state, or the college itself, and do not require repayment. They are usually awarded based on need, merit, or both.

Work-Study: This is a federal program that provides part-time jobs for students who qualify for financial assistance, enabling them to earn money to help cover education expenses.

Loans: These funds must be repaid with interest. Subsidized loans have government-paid interest while in school, while unsubsidized loans do not.

Read The Fine Print: It is essential to review all the aid package details, including terms and conditions. If offered loans, paying attention to the interest rate, commencement of repayment, and loan term is crucial. These factors significantly impact the total amount repaid over time.

Distinguish Between Gift Aid & Borrowed Money: Not all financial aid is created equal. Grants and scholarships are frequently called "gift aid" because no repayment is required. On the other hand, loans are borrowed money that accrues interest and must be repaid.

Understand Your Expected Family Contribution (EFC): The EFC serves as an index number colleges use to assess financial aid eligibility. It does not represent the amount families must pay for college or the federal student aid students will receive. Instead, it is a figure schools use to determine eligibility for financial aid.

Calculate Your Net Cost: This is the cost of attendance (COA) minus total grants and scholarships. The COA includes tuition, fees, room and board, books, supplies, and other expenses. The net cost represents the total amount to be covered by income, savings, or loans.

Ask Questions: If you need more clarification on any aspect of your financial aid package, consider contacting the college's office of financial assistance. It is essential to be clear on what is being accepted.

Building A Safety Net: Savings & Emergency Funds

Life can be unpredictable, but being prepared is your strongest ally. This is especially true when it comes to managing finances. It is easy for a busy first-year student to overlook the importance of savings and having an emergency fund.

Savings: These provide a financial cushion for plans, goals, and even whims. The fund can support a much-needed break, a spontaneous road trip, or a course you have always wanted to take. More importantly, savings can protect against debt, ensuring that borrowing is unnecessary for every unexpected expense or opportunity.

Emergency Fund: Such a fund is an essential part of saving money. It acts like a "safety net" for unexpected expenditures, such as sudden medical bills, major car repairs, or unexpected tuition fee hikes. Having an emergency fund helps avoid financial trouble if these unforeseen situations occur.

Here are some practical ways to save money and seamlessly incorporate these practices into college life.

Set A Savings Goal: Following the earlier section on budgeting, decide on a realistic amount that can be saved from excess monthly income or allowance. Even small amounts can add up over time.

Open A Separate Savings Account: This helps separate everyday spending from savings. Look for an account with low fees and a competitive interest rate.

Automate Savings: If possible, set up automatic transfers to a savings account. This way, you can save money without even thinking about it.

Build An Emergency Fund: Aim to save enough to cover three to six months of living expenses. It may seem like a lot, but don't let this discourage you. The aim is to gradually build up the fund, not to save all at once.

Limit Access To Your Emergency Fund: To ensure the money is only used in genuine times of need and to prevent temptation or misuse, introducing additional barriers to accessing the funds could be beneficial. A viable solution is setting up a separate account dedicated to the emergency fund from the primary savings account. These limitations provide more time to reconsider and help avoid unnecessary expenditures.

Choose a different bank or financial institution from your primary bank.

Select an account that does not offer a debit card or easy online access.

Pick a savings account with advance notice requirements for withdrawals or one with tiered interest rates for maintaining specific balances.

Adjust As Needed: Review savings goals and amounts periodically. As income or expenses fluctuate, your savings strategy should adapt accordingly.

By incorporating savings and an emergency fund into financial habits, one is not just preparing for unexpected events but also establishing a solid foundation for the future. Remember, the objective is not solely about having money but about attaining financial security, flexibility, and peace of mind.

Managing Student Debt

Students must thoroughly understand debt, including its implications, management, and eventual elimination. Managing debt, whether student loans, credit card bills, or personal loans, is no small task. It involves understanding obligations, budgeting wisely, setting up a repayment plan, and maintaining sound financial habits.

Ignoring debt will not make it disappear! It can worsen the situation, making it harder to recover financially later. Remember, managing debt is not just about paying off what is owed but also about cultivating good financial habits. Successfully doing this requires discipline, patience, and perseverance.

Understand Your Debt: Know the institutions owed, how much, the interest rates, and the repayment terms. Create a list or a spreadsheet of all debts, including all loans (student and personal) and credit cards, repayment amounts, interest, and terms and conditions.

Create A Budget: As already outlined, develop a realistic budget that covers necessities such as rent, food, and utilities, as well as debt repayments. Track all income and expenses. Doing so can provide insights into where money is being spent and help identify areas where savings can be made.

Prioritize Your Debts: Not all debts are the same. Those with higher interest rates can snowball and should usually be prioritized for repayment first. If unable to pay off more, keep making at least minimum payments on all debts to avoid penalties.

Timely Payments: Always pay bills on time. Late payments can result in additional fees and higher interest rates and negatively affect credit scores. Consider setting up automatic payments if you are concerned about forgetting due dates.

Emergency Fund: Having resources to fund the unexpected can help cover expenses without borrowing more money. Even a small amount saved each month can make a big difference.

Explore Payment Plans & Forgiveness Programs: Income-driven repayment plans or loan forgiveness programs may be available for federal student loans. Research these and consider seeking advice from a financial advisor to gain insights into available options.

Avoid Unnecessary Debt: It may be tempting to use a credit card for non-essential items or take out additional loans, but this can lead to a cycle of increasing debt. So stay within your budget and, crucially, live within your means.

The Benefits & Dangers Of Credit Cards

A credit card can seem like a magic wand – a small, plastic ticket to freedom, granting the power to buy now and pay later. While it brings convenience and helps build credit history, a credit card also comes with responsibilities and potential pitfalls that, if ignored, can lead to financial difficulties.

Here, we explore the world of credit cards and demystify terms like credit limit, interest rate, and minimum payment. We will also delve into how a credit card works and can include perks, such as rewards and cash back, as well as risks, like high interest and debt.

Credit cards must be viewed not as an extension of your wallet but as a financial tool to be wielded with caution and respect. It is essential to understand that owning a credit card involves more than just making purchases. It also requires managing debt, avoiding unnecessary charges, and building a solid credit history. A credit card can be a stepping stone to financial freedom or a stumbling block leading to debt; the choice is yours. Let's ensure it becomes the former.

Credit Card Terms

It is essential to understand the standard terms associated with credit cards. A credit card functions as a type of loan, typically charging a higher interest rate than a traditional bank loan. Let's break these terms down:

Credit Limit: This is the maximum balance that can be borrowed for spending from a credit card company or financial institution. Staying comfortably below this limit is crucial, as reaching or exceeding it can adversely affect your credit score.

Balance: This is the amount owed to the credit card company. This includes purchases, cash advances, balance transfers, fees, and accrued interest.

Cash Advance: This is when a credit card is used to withdraw cash, but it often comes with high interest rates and fees, making it an expensive way to borrow money.

Minimum Payment: This is the lowest amount that can be paid on the monthly credit card balance to keep the account in good standing. While paying the lowest amount may avoid late penalties, it does not prevent the accumulation of interest on the unpaid balance. Hence, paying off the entire balance is recommended to avoid interest charges.

Interest Rate (APR): APR stands for Annual Percentage Rate and signifies the borrowing cost associated with the card if the monthly balance is not fully paid off. It is represented as a yearly rate. Cards with a high APR can swiftly accumulate substantial debt, particularly if only minimum payments are made.

Grace Period: This is the date from the end of a billing cycle to the payment due date, during which no interest accrues. The grace period typically only applies if the outstanding amount is paid in full each month.

Late Payment Penalty Fee: A late payment fee can be charged if the minimum amount is not paid by the due date. Late payments can also adversely impact credit scores.

Rewards: Many credit cards offer rewards programs, including cashback, points, or travel miles. However, cards with substantial rewards often have higher interest rates or annual fees.

Annual Fee: Some (not all) credit cards charge a yearly fee for use, which is added to the balance on the card. In return, these cards often provide rewards or other benefits. It is essential to evaluate whether the benefits outweigh the cost of the fee.

Credit Card Benefits

Credit cards are not only about borrowing money. When used wisely, they can come with different benefits that could save money and provide valuable conveniences. As benefits vary, it is essential to determine which types of benefits your card offers. Here are some key benefits commonly offered by credit cards:

Rewards Programs: Many offer rewards, points, cash back, or miles for every dollar spent. Over time, these points can add up and be redeemed for benefits such as travel, gift cards, or even as a credit on your account. Understanding how a card's rewards program works is essential to maximize the benefits.

Building Credit History / Good Credit Score: Regular and responsible credit card use helps to build a strong credit history. This can be advantageous for loan submissions, apartment rentals, or job applications.

Purchase Protection: Some cards cover the cost of items bought on the card if stolen or damaged within a specific time frame. Terms and conditions can vary, so it is worth checking what protections a card offers.

Extended Warranties: A credit card company may extend the manufacturer's warranty on certain purchases. This could save money if an item purchased with the card breaks or becomes faulty.

Travel Insurance: Some policies cover travel, including trip cancellation, lost luggage, or medical emergencies. If you are a frequent traveler, these benefits can save the need to buy separate insurance.

Fraud Protection: Most cards have zero liability cover, where cardholders aren't responsible for unauthorized charges if the card is lost or stolen.

Convenience: Credit cards are widely accepted and provide a secure and convenient alternative to cash or checks.

Credit Card Pitfalls

While credit cards can offer many advantages, they can pose serious risks if not used responsibly. Below are potential hazards to keep in mind:

High Interest Rates: These cards often charge high interest rates, especially for cash advances or for those with lower credit scores. Not paying off the full balance every month can lead to rapid accumulation of interest, resulting in rising debt that may become difficult to manage.

Late Payment Penalties: Failure to pay the minimum amount by the due date will result in late fees being charged. Late payments can also negatively impact credit scores. Note that these late fees are in addition to the interest paid on the outstanding balance.

Overuse & Overspending: Owning a credit card can lead to the temptation to overspend, particularly on impulsive or non-essential purchases. This can quickly lead to unmanageable debt.

Impact On Credit Score: Frequently maxing out the card or carrying a high balance can lower your credit score, affecting your ability to obtain loans or other credit in the future. The credit score is influenced by payment history and credit utilization, which refers to the amount owed on the card compared to the credit limit.

Debt Spiral: Only making minimum monthly payments can lead to rising debt. Since minimum payments typically cover only the interest and a small portion of the outstanding balance, this debt can take years to pay off and cost much more in interest.

Fraud Risk: If card information falls into the wrong hands, it can be used to make fraudulent purchases. While most credit cards have zero-liability policies for fraudulent charges, dealing with credit card fraud can be time-consuming and stressful.

Beware Of Credit Card Offers

A student might be inundated with credit card offers, often promising attractive rewards or perks. However, it is essential to approach these offers with caution. While a credit card can be a handy tool for managing finances and building a credit history, it also comes with potential drawbacks. As outlined above, credit cards typically have high interest rates, and it is easy to fall into debt if the balance is not paid off each month. Furthermore, some credit cards have hefty annual fees, late payment penalties, and complex terms and conditions.

If not carefully managed, these factors can outweigh any initial incentives. Therefore, before accepting any credit card offer, it is vital to read the fine print, understand the interest rates, fees, and charges, compare card offers, and consider whether owning a credit card is manageable. A credit card is a tool, so its safety depends on how responsibly it is used.

Understanding the Importance of Your Credit Score

A student managing finances independently often involves opening a bank account or applying for a credit card. Amid these crucial steps, your credit score or report can profoundly impact your financial journey.

This is like a report card for your finances. In the US, it is a three-digit number that banks, lenders, and sometimes landlords or employers look at to assess an individual's past financial conduct. In essence, a credit score reflects financial reliability based on borrowing history, loan repayment, punctual bill payments, and debt management. Lenders, landlords, and sometimes even employers look at this score to gauge a person's trustworthiness in financial matters.

To maintain a good credit score, ensure on-time repayment of borrowed funds. A good, high credit score can make it easier and cheaper to borrow money. It can unlock doors to lower interest rates on loans, better chances of rental application approvals, lower insurance premiums, and improved credit card terms. Conversely, those who have paid late or accumulated excessive debt will likely have a lower score, making it more difficult to access the above benefits. Therefore, it is vital to keep this score high by making timely bill payments, borrowing sensibly, and regularly reviewing credit reports for accuracy and awareness of your financial standing.

Does A Credit Score Have A Set Life span?

A credit score does not have an expiration date or a fixed lifespan. It is an evolving number that changes over time based on the information in the credit report. This dynamic number reflects borrowing and repayment history, current debt levels, and other factors.

The data in a credit report, however, does have a limited duration. Negative information, such as late payments and defaults, typically remains on the report for seven years, while bankruptcy can last ten years. Positive data, such as on-time payments and low balances, can stay on the report indefinitely, eventually leading to an improved credit score. Note that while old information does fall off the report eventually, having sound financial habits is vital to maintaining a healthy credit score.

The key takeaway is that a credit score is much more than just a number. It reflects your financial behavior and credibility, affecting many aspects of your life. It can be a safety net, providing access to funds during emergencies. In essence, maintaining a good credit score opens a world of opportunities. Therefore, managing finances responsibly is not just recommended but essential for long-term financial well-being.

Generating Income: Ways To Fund Your Education

As tuition costs continue to rise, finding ways to pay for college without taking on debt becomes increasingly important. Here are some options:

Scholarships

Many scholarships are available based on academic performance, athletic ability, leadership involvement, and more. Additionally, some scholarships are specifically designed for certain fields of study or individuals from particular backgrounds. Students should apply for as many scholarships as possible, as every bit counts!

Grants

Unlike loans, grants do not require repayment. They can come from federal or state governments, colleges, or private or nonprofit organizations. Grants are typically given based on financial need, though some may also consider academic achievement or other factors.

Research what grants are available in your region. For US students, start by completing the Free Application for Federal Student Aid (FAFSA) provided by the U.S. Department of Education. This form determines eligibility for federal grants, which many state and institutional grants also require. Contact the financial aid office or check the college website for more details on grants available to you.

Professional associations, corporations, and nonprofit organizations often offer grants for specific fields of study or students from particular backgrounds, so research online for these opportunities. Additionally, explore trusted websites such as College Board's Scholarship Search, Fastweb, or Grants.gov for further options within the US. Be thorough in your search and apply for as many eligible grants as possible, but remain cautious of scams – legitimate grants should never require payment for application or provision of information.

Work-Study Programs

Certain programs, funded by the federal government and sometimes by the state, enable students to earn money for their education. These programs mainly offer part-time work on campus, which is convenient for the students. The jobs offered are usually course-related or serve the public in some manner, thus providing valuable work experience in addition to financial aid. The money earned from these work-study jobs is typically used to pay for tuition, books, and living expenses.

First, complete the FAFSA and indicate your interest in work-study on the application to learn about work-study programs. Then, contact the college financial aid office to verify eligibility and discover available work-study jobs. Each college may have different processes and application deadlines, so staying proactive and informed is crucial.

For international students or those studying outside the US, inquire with your institution's financial aid office or student services department about similar opportunities available to you. They may offer their own work-study programs or alternative forms of student employment to assist with educational expenses.

Part-Time Work or Internships

College students can benefit in two ways from part-time jobs. Firstly, they can use the income earned from their job to cover their college expenses. Secondly, part-time jobs provide practical opportunities to improve skills, gain experience, and grow a professional network. This experience and network can be highly valuable when searching for a job after graduation. In essence, part-time work and internships help manage the financial strain of college while providing valuable experience that enhances competitiveness in the job market after graduation.

Part-time jobs come in various shapes and sizes. On-campus jobs may include work in the university library, dining hall, or admissions office. These jobs often offer flexibility with hours to accommodate class schedules. Off-campus jobs could include retail, food service, tutoring, or other roles. The aim is to maintain a healthy balance between work, academic responsibilities, and personal time. Remember, while earning money is important, your primary role as a student is to study and excel academically.

Internships are temporary positions companies and organizations offer to students or recent graduates. They are often closely related to one's field of study or future career goals, providing hands-on experience in a particular industry or role. Although not all internships are paid, the experience gained can be highly valuable. Internships allow students to apply theories learned in the classroom to real-world situations, better understand workplace dynamics, and establish connections in their desired field.

It is worth noting that the college careers office can be an excellent resource for finding part-time jobs and internships. They can help with job listings, resume building, interview preparation, and connecting with alumni or other professionals in the chosen field.

Crowdfunding

This is an innovative approach leveraging social networks to gather small donations from many people. Creating a campaign on sites like GoFundMe, Kickstarter, or Indiegogo involves setting a fundraising goal and asking for donations from family, friends, and strangers by sharing your story. This can be useful for funding specific projects or opportunities, such as study abroad programs, research projects, or unexpected educational expenses. While crowdfunding can be a great tool, success depends on effectively conveying needs and goals and successfully promoting the campaign, for example, through social media channels. Be aware of the fees charged by these platforms, as they might deduct a percentage of the funds raised.

Family Support

If your family is willing and able to help with college costs, this can be a valuable funding source. It is essential to have open and honest conversations about finances and to set clear expectations.

Savings

These funds may come from savings accounts established by parents or guardians during childhood or from income earned from part-time or summer jobs during high school and college. Using savings for college costs can be a wise strategy, as it avoids interest charges from loans. However, you must budget carefully and ensure that savings are used efficiently and strategically. Also, maintain an emergency fund to allow for unexpected expenses. Ideally, combining savings with other forms of funding, such as scholarships, grants, and work-study opportunities, can maximize financial resources for college.

Remember, every small amount counts. Start the search for financial aid early, apply for as many eligible grants and scholarships as possible, and consider various forms of employment. Begin saving as early as possible. With careful planning and persistence, securing funding for college without accruing unnecessary debt is possible.

The importance of money management for a student cannot be overstated. This period serves as the introduction to adulthood, where financial decisions can profoundly impact your future. Understanding how to budget, save, invest, manage debt, and make informed financial decisions can mean the difference between graduating with a comfortable financial safety net or a burdensome load of debt. It is not just about making ends meet but also about setting the groundwork for long-term financial health. Remember, every decision made, however small it may seem, shapes this financial journey. So, take control, stay informed, and cultivate healthy financial habits!

Chapter 12

Planting The Seeds Of Success For The Future

" The future depends on what you do today."

Mahatma Gandhi

Preparing For Your Future

Your time at college is precious. These may be your final carefree days as a student before assuming the life of a fully working adult. It is essential to appreciate that the choices made during this time can significantly impact your future.

Today, more than just a degree is needed to guarantee success. Employers are looking for a blend of education, skills, and experiences that can be acquired during college. This chapter provides guidance on maximizing your college years and preparing for life afterward. From honing study habits to engaging in various extracurricular activities, there are numerous strategies to ensure that your time at college is rewarding and productive. With focused planning and preparation, these years can serve as a foundation for long-term success.

Cultivating A Growth Mindset

A growth mindset is vital to making the most of college and life after graduation. It involves understanding and adopting a positive approach to life, including:

- Improvements and growth are achievable with effort and dedication.

- Challenges are to be embraced and viewed as opportunities to learn.

- Being fearless of taking on unfamiliar responsibilities.

- Failures should not be seen as setbacks but as chances to improve.

Approaching studying, extracurricular activities, and internships with this mindset means being more receptive to exploring new experiences, expanding skillsets, and gaining further knowledge. It results in resilience in the face of challenges and encourages persistence until goals are achieved, traits highly valued in the job market.

But how can this growth mindset be cultivated? It begins with acknowledging that intelligence and skills are not fixed but can be developed. Do not be discouraged; instead, embrace challenges as learning opportunities rather than obstacles. Focus on continuous improvement instead of immediate outcomes.

Maintaining a growth mindset will equip you to handle life's inevitable ups and downs and prepare you for the ever-changing job market. It also encourages a passion for learning, resilience in adversity, and determination to achieve goals.

Defining Your Vision For The Future & Setting Goals

Having goals is crucial, whether now or in the future. Goals can provide a roadmap to help manage academic and extracurricular activities. It is important to have both short-term goals, such as completing an assignment or project, and long-term goals, such as pursuing a particular career. Having a clear vision of what needs to be achieved can help you focus on relevant opportunities and position yourself effectively for life after graduation.

What Do You Like Doing? Before deciding on the future, consider your interests, strengths, and passions. What do you love to do? What are your natural talents? Are there subjects or activities that you find so engaging that you lose track of time? You can craft a better vision for a future that reflects your ambitions and aspirations by answering these questions.

What Type Of Job Interests You? As this vision is developed, consider the potential career path. Reflect on the type of work you see yourself doing after graduation. A career that directly uses your major or combines multiple areas of interest could be suitable. Aligning career aspirations with college experience would be ideal, as this will help tailor academic and extracurricular participation to gain relevant skills and experiences.

Plan How To Get There: Keeping this vision and potential career in mind, set specific, measurable, achievable, relevant, and time-bound (SMART) goals. For example, for a career as a software developer, an aim could be to learn a new programming language each semester. This aligns with your career goal and develops relevant skills for your intended career.

Achieving a vision is a gradual process that requires setting milestones in the form of goals. Working towards these goals during college requires taking proactive steps toward building this envisioned future. This approach makes the most of your time at college and paves the way toward your desired career.

Know Your Strengths, Weaknesses & Passions

Knowing these helps to provide a foundation for personal and professional development and can guide decisions during college and beyond.

Strengths: These are the areas where you naturally excel. They could be specific skills, such as writing or problem-solving, or personal traits, like leadership or creativity. Recognizing these strengths can steer your academic direction and select relevant internships, eventually leading to a career that effectively harnesses your abilities.

Weaknesses: Understanding these provides an opportunity for self-improvement. Perhaps you need help with time management, public speaking, or a specific academic subject. Rather than avoiding these areas, college offers the perfect environment to work on them. Remember, employers are looking for well-rounded individuals who continually strive for improvement. So, use college resources such as tutoring centers and workshops to turn these weaknesses into strengths.

Passions: These are activities you genuinely love to do. They bring joy and satisfaction, feeling more like hobbies than chores. Identifying these passions can guide you toward a fulfilling career path where you can excel. Whether art, research, helping others, or solving complex problems, your passions can lead to success.

Throughout college, leverage your strengths, work on weaknesses, and pursue your passions, laying the groundwork for a successful post-graduation life.

Leveraging Extracurricular Activities for Personal Growth

Extracurricular activities are pivotal in enhancing college life and personal growth. These activities range from sports and student bodies to clubs, volunteer work, and internships. They provide excellent opportunities to explore interests outside the classroom, develop new skills, and make valuable connections. Participating in these activities enables students to apply what they were taught in class and, perhaps more importantly, learn what cannot be taught in class, such as teamwork, leadership, time management, and other forms of problem-solving.

Discover What Is Offered: Explore the various extracurricular activities available at college. Choose ones that align with your interests, goals, and passions. For instance, if you are interested in journalism, consider joining the college newspaper. If social service is your passion, volunteering in community outreach programs can be a great fit. Remember, the goal is not to fill your resume with a long list of activities but to deeply engage in a few that truly matter to you. This level of engagement helps the development of skills and experiences that employers find valuable.

Networking Opportunities: Extracurricular activities also provide an avenue for networking, allowing interaction with peers, faculty, and industry professionals. These relationships can be invaluable for personal development, providing mentorship, learning from others' experiences, and potentially opening doors to job opportunities in the future.

Remember that the lessons and experiences gained from extracurricular involvement can be as important as academic achievements in preparing for life after graduation.

Building A Solid Academic Foundation

Your academic foundation will be the bedrock upon which you build your career, so it is essential to take it seriously. A solid educational background is about more than just achieving good grades, although that is undoubtedly important. It also means understanding the chosen field of study, developing critical thinking skills, and expanding the knowledge base.

Make Full Use Of All Resources: Take full advantage of the resources and opportunities available at college. Attend classes regularly, participate actively, and always seek help or ask questions when needed. Use office hours with professors who can provide valuable insights and guidance. Use the library, online resources, and study groups to deepen your understanding of the course material. The more engaged you are with your studies, the stronger your academic foundation will be.

Choose Courses & Projects That Support Future Goals: Take a strategic approach to your education by selecting courses and projects that align with future career goals. Make sure the courses complement your major and add depth to your knowledge. Engage fully with the material and use every opportunity to learn. Participate in class, ask questions, and explore the subject matter deeply. Work on a project to help build expertise in your field of interest. By doing so, you will develop critical thinking skills, effective communication, and problem-solving abilities highly valued by employers in all industries.

Broaden Overall Knowledge: While it is essential to delve deeply into your major, take courses in other disciplines as well. This interdisciplinary approach to learning can foster creativity and innovation, making you a more versatile and attractive candidate in the job market. It can also provide exposure to different perspectives and ideas, which can benefit any career. For business majors, for example, taking courses in environmental science or sustainability can provide insights into corporate social responsibility and eco-friendly business practices. The skills and knowledge gained can make you a more socially conscious and competitive candidate in the business world.

Challenge Yourself Academically: Take on tasks that push you intellectually. These might include writing a thesis, working as a teaching assistant, or undertaking a research project. These experiences reinforce your academic foundation and develop critical research, communication, and leadership skills. They are also tangible achievements that can be highlighted to future employers.

Remember, building a solid academic foundation in college is more than just earning a degree; it is about developing a well-rounded knowledge base and skills to support your future career.

What If I Don't Have A Career In Mind Yet?

There is no need to worry if you are undecided about a future career. Instead, the approach to course and project selection can be about exploring interests, building versatile skills, and keeping options open.

Choose Courses Across Different Fields Of Interest: This will provide a broader educational experience and exposure to various potential career paths. You may find a subject not previously considered to be surprisingly captivating, which could lead to a new career interest. For example, a business major could take an introductory course in psychology just out of curiosity. This could lead to discovering the fascinating subject of human behavior and how understanding people's motivations and behavior can be incredibly useful in a business setting. This could lead to career paths combining these areas, such as human resources, marketing, organizational psychology, or behavioral finance.

Develop Versatile Skills: Choose projects that enhance transferable skills such as critical thinking, communication, problem-solving, and leadership, which are valuable in almost any career. Engaging in projects challenging and pushing beyond your comfort zone can foster these skills. Working on a team project can enhance collaboration and leadership qualities, while a research project might sharpen analytical and problem-solving skills.

Remember that goals and interests may evolve, and flexibility is always necessary. The experiences and knowledge acquired can all influence your career path. So, keep an open mind, seize opportunities, and know that every experience is valuable in shaping your future.

Graduate School: Is This The Right Path For You?

Whether or not to pursue further education after graduation is a significant decision that can impact your career path and future. Also, it is not the right choice for everyone. The choice should be based on carefully considering career aspirations, interests, and the realities of your chosen field.

Consider Your Career Goals: Does your chosen career require, or would it significantly benefit from, an advanced degree? For instance, a graduate degree is necessary if the goal is to be a clinical psychologist or a university professor. However, relevant work experience might be valued more than an advanced degree for a career in tech or certain business roles. Therefore, it is essential to research the norms and expectations of your chosen field.

Time & Money: Graduate school is a considerable investment of time, effort, and often money. You must realistically consider your readiness for this commitment and the challenges that come with it. Are you genuinely passionate about diving deeper into your field of study? Do you have the academic preparation and stamina needed for rigorous advanced studies? Are you financially prepared or willing to seek scholarships or assistantships? These are critical questions to reflect on.

Ultimately, the decision to attend graduate school should align with personal and career goals and be a step you are excited about and ready to take.

Developing Transferable Skills For The Future

Transferable skills, often called 'soft skills,' can be applied to many jobs and industries. Examples include good communication, the ability to work effectively in a team, problem-solving, and the ability to organize and plan well. These skills can be used in almost any job, from a business manager to a teacher to a software engineer. By contrast, hard skills are specific to a particular job or field and not applicable across other industries (such as coding for a software engineer or being able to draw blood for a nurse!).

Transferable skills are essential because they help you adapt to different roles and responsibilities during your career. Today, it is not uncommon for someone to switch careers several times. Having a solid set of transferable skills can make these transitions easier.

Employers also value these skills highly. When they hire, they are not only looking for someone with the technical skills to do the job. They also want someone who can work well with others, solve problems, and communicate effectively. So, in essence, robust transferable skills can make you a more competitive candidate.

Skills Often Valued By Employers & How To Acquire Them

Transferable skills are highly sought after by many employers across various industries. While specific skills needed can vary depending on the job, some general types are universally beneficial. Here are some suggestions for developing these skills during college.

Communication: The capability to convey ideas clearly and effectively in writing and verbally is crucial in nearly all fields. This includes listening, understanding, and responding effectively to others.

How To Acquire: Join a debate club, participate actively in class discussions, write for the college newspaper, or present at student conferences. Each activity can help refine your ability to express ideas clearly and effectively.

Problem-Solving: Employers value those who can think analytically and critically, make decisions, and solve problems.

How To Acquire: Engage in research projects, participate in case competitions, or undertake internships or courses that involve complex projects. These activities require identifying problems, developing solutions, and making decisions.

Teamwork & Collaboration: Most jobs involve working with others in some capacity. Effective teamwork, as well as cooperating and negotiating with others, is highly valued in the workplace.

How To Acquire: Join a club or organization, participate in group projects, or play team sports. These experiences provide opportunities to work with others towards a common goal and can help you learn to navigate group dynamics effectively.

Leadership: Even if you are not in a management role, the ability to lead, inspire, motivate others, and take responsibility for tasks are valuable qualities.

How To Acquire: Take on leadership roles in student organizations, volunteer for a lead role in group projects, or mentor younger students. Such experiences allow you to practice guiding others and making decisions.

Organizational: These include managing time effectively, prioritizing tasks, and working efficiently. These skills are essential for meeting deadlines and managing workloads in a professional setting.

How To Acquire: Balance academics with part-time jobs, internships, or extracurricular activities. This can help you learn to manage your time effectively, prioritize tasks, and stay organized.

Adaptability & Flexibility: Being amenable and open to change is essential in a fast-paced, ever-changing work environment.

How to Acquire: Study abroad, take interdisciplinary courses, or take on projects that challenge beyond your comfort level. These experiences can teach you how to adapt to new environments and challenges.

Digital Literacy: Being comfortable with technology and digital platforms is vital in the modern workplace. It can range from basic computer abilities to more specialized knowledge, such as understanding data analytics or digital marketing.

How To Acquire: Take computer science or digital media courses or get involved in projects that require technology. Learn to touch-type. This can help you become comfortable with digital platforms and enhance your technical capabilities.

Innovation & Creativity: Being able to think outside the box and develop innovative solutions are skills that can set you apart from others.

How To Acquire: Participate in creative activities, such as art or writing clubs, or take courses encouraging innovative thinking. This can help you learn to think creatively when generating new ideas.

Leverage College Workshops

Many colleges offer seminars and workshops to help students develop these soft skills. These can cover various topics, from communication and leadership to time management and critical thinking. Experienced professionals or faculty members often facilitate them and can provide practical, hands-on training.

For instance, a workshop on public speaking can help enhance communication and presentation skills, while a seminar on conflict resolution can improve problem-solving and teamwork abilities. Similarly, participating in a time management workshop can boost organization and efficiency, and attending a digital literacy seminar can teach new software or digital tools relevant to your field of study.

Attending these workshops not only helps you acquire and polish new skills, but also allows you to expand your perspective and network by meeting other students with similar interests.

Why Work Experience Is Important

Work experience provides an opportunity to apply academic knowledge in a real-world setting, deepening understanding of the desired career path or field of study. It also fosters the development and refining of vital transferable skills such as communication, teamwork, problem-solving, and time management, which are valued across all industries.

In today's competitive job market, having relevant work experience while still at college is increasingly important. It is no longer just a nice-to-have but often a requirement employers look for when assessing potential candidates. Work experience, whether an internship, part-time job, co-op role, or even volunteering, provides practical skills beyond what is learned in a classroom. It offers a firsthand understanding of the working world and can help a smoother transition from student life to a professional environment.

Work experience can facilitate informed career decisions. It allows the exploration of different roles and industries, helping to identify preferences and strengths. If the experience was not what was expected or enjoyed, it would enable the reassessment of your career path. Plus, it is a chance to start building a professional network, which can prove invaluable when ready to enter the job market.

In essence, gaining work experience during college can provide a competitive edge after graduation. It provides valuable practical skills, assists in identifying career goals, and enables networking with professionals in the relevant field. Therefore, it is recommended to proactively seek and take advantage of work opportunities during college, as this can significantly impact your career journey.

Types Of Work Experience

Internships: These are typically short-term work experiences companies and organizations offer to expose students to a particular industry or field. They can be paid or unpaid, sometimes leading to a job offer after graduation. They are usually undertaken during summer breaks or as part of academic programs, providing students with valuable real-world experience. Internships enable the application of the theoretical knowledge gained in class, the appreciation of that profession's day-to-day operations, and the development of industry-specific skills.

Part-Time Jobs: Whether on campus or off, part-time jobs can provide experience in areas such as customer service, time management, and undertaking responsibility. While these may not directly relate to your desired career, the skills gained can be valuable in any job.

Co-op Programs: Some colleges offer co-operative education programs, which allow alternating semesters of academic study and full-time employment in the relevant field. These programs can provide in-depth industry experience and valuable connections.

Research Positions: If considering a career in academia or a science-related field, working as a research assistant can provide a taste of what is involved. Through this role, skills acquired include data collection, analysis, critical thinking, and potentially contributing to published papers.

Volunteering: Volunteer work in the local community or through opportunities abroad can provide valuable experiences while making a positive impact. It can also help demonstrate desired qualities such as empathy, teamwork, and leadership.

Freelance Work Or Entrepreneurship: Flexible freelance work, such as graphic design or programming, can provide valuable knowledge. Similarly, starting a small business can provide marketing, sales, finance, business management and entrepreneurship experience.

Gaining work experience in college can enhance your resume, setting you apart from other candidates by demonstrating practical exposure to the working world. It offers insights into your preferred type of work and the environments in which you thrive, all while making valuable industry connections. It also starts building your professional network, which can lead to post-graduation job opportunities. Therefore, seize these opportunities to gain work experience while in college.

Studying Abroad Programs & Travel Opportunities

In today's interconnected world, a global perspective can significantly enhance your competitiveness and readiness for post-college life. And what better way to cultivate this perspective than through travel opportunities? As a student, you may have access to study abroad programs, international internships, or simply traveling during breaks. Embracing these opportunities can broaden your worldview, deepen cultural understanding, and prepare you for a career in the global economy. It is also an invaluable way to develop a range of transferable skills. Therefore, investigating these opportunities while in college is well worth doing.

Benefits Of International Travel

New Customs & Cultures: Immersion into new ways of life helps to develop an appreciation for diversity and the ability to interact effectively with people from different cultural backgrounds. Many employers, especially those with international operations or clients, highly value this cultural sensitivity.

Language Skills: Travel can introduce new languages or enable you to practice existing linguistic skills. Even if you are not fluent in a country's language, trying to communicate can be a valuable learning experience. Many employers value multilingual abilities and view them as a sign of adaptability and willingness to learn.

Transferable Skills: Travel helps cultivate numerous invaluable soft skills in your personal and professional life. When traveling, especially alone or within a study program, unexpected challenges are often encountered. Navigating these situations develops problem-solving, adaptability, resilience, and decision-making skills.

Communication Skills: Engaging with locals and fellow students from different backgrounds refines effective expression and understanding. It cultivates the ability to articulate ideas clearly and fosters better understanding, especially when language barriers exist.

Independence: During travel, self-reliance is crucial. Managing day-to-day life in a new country, from navigating foreign transportation systems to budget management, can significantly boost confidence and initiative, both valued traits in any professional setting.

Adaptability & Resilience: Traveling abroad, especially for studying or internships, fosters flexibility, resilience, and open-mindedness. Adapting to new customs, languages, and cultures enhances these qualities, making you a more desirable candidate for employers.

Problem-Solving Abilities: Navigating daily life in an unfamiliar environment presents challenges that demand quick thinking and innovative problem-solving. This enhances critical thinking and decision-making abilities.

Broadens Career Horizons: Immersion in a different culture and environment can lead to discovering new interests, innovative ideas, or unique career paths. Local professionals or researchers may offer fresh perspectives that could inspire career decisions.

Job Opportunities: The global network built while overseas can lead to international job opportunities, providing a broader perspective and diversified professional options. This network becomes a vital asset when starting the job search after graduation.

International Networking: The people you meet abroad could become lifelong friends, future colleagues, or valuable professional connections. This network can offer various opportunities and insights down the road that would otherwise be inaccessible.

Embracing travel opportunities can significantly enhance your life experience and personal growth. Travel broadens horizons and equips you with unique skills that are difficult to acquire in a classroom setting. So, if the chance to travel arises, seize it!

Uncovering Opportunities To Travel

Travel opportunities for students may not seem easily accessible. However, many resources and options are available. The key is to be open, curious, and proactive in seeking these opportunities.

Internships Or Volunteering Abroad: These can offer enriching experiences and professional growth opportunities. If your course of study allows, consider seeking an internship abroad to gain valuable experience and exposure to a new culture. Similarly, volunteering abroad can provide meaningful experiences and contribute to personal development. Numerous organizations facilitate internships and volunteer opportunities abroad.

For example, AIESEC is a well-known non-profit organization that offers leadership development, cross-cultural internships, and global volunteer exchange experiences, which are available to students worldwide.

Study Abroad Programs: Your college or university likely has a study abroad office or international programs department. Visit their office, check their website, or attend information sessions to gain valuable insights on what is available, countries to visit, and the application process. Additionally, they often share inspiring stories of past students' experiences, which can help you make informed decisions.

College Departments & Clubs: Keeping an eye on communication from your college departments or clubs is essential. They frequently organize trips or events related to their field of interest. Participating in these trips offers an excellent opportunity to travel, learn, and connect with peers with similar interests.

Online Resources: Websites such as GoAbroad.com or StudyAbroad.com provide extensive information on various international programs, destinations, and fields of study. They enable comparison and assist in selecting the best opportunity for you.

Networking: Speak to seniors, alumni, professors, or career advisors who can share their experiences, insights, and advice. Also connect with students from different countries to learn about their culture and potential opportunities in their home countries.

Can Stay "Local": Remember, traveling does not necessarily mean the need to cross the ocean. Start by exploring different cities, states, or provinces within your country. Each place offers a unique perspective and enriches your overall experience.

Funding Your Travels

Financing study abroad programs, internships, or travel experiences can be a significant concern for many students. However, there are various avenues to consider that can provide financial support. It is recommended to research and apply to multiple places to increase the chances of securing funding for international adventures. Here are a few resources to consider:

Financial Aid & Scholarships: Check with your university's office for financial assistance or study abroad office to determine if your current financial aid package can be applied to study abroad programs. Also, many colleges and universities offer scholarships for this kind of travel. Look at your institution's website or visit an advisor to learn about these opportunities.

Program-Specific Scholarships: Many programs offer specific scholarships or grants. Check the program's website or speak with a program representative to learn what financial aid they may offer.

International Fellowships & Grants: Many educational institutions, non-profit organizations, and foundations worldwide provide fellowships or grants specifically for international study abroad, travel, or research opportunities. Programs such as the Fulbright Program and Rhodes Scholarships are prestigious examples. Additionally, your college or university may have unique offerings for its own students.

External Scholarships & Grants: Numerous organizations and foundations offer scholarships and grants for studying and international experiences. For example, the Benjamin A. Gilman International Scholarship Program provides grants for U.S. students studying abroad, and the Fund for Education Abroad awards scholarships to students participating in high-quality, rigorous education abroad programs. International students should research and explore opportunities from various organizations specific to their home countries or regions.

Crowdfunding & Fundraising: If traditional scholarships and grants are not enough or unavailable, consider raising money through crowdfunding websites like GoFundMe or FundMyTravel. Share your story and fundraising campaign with friends, family, and social media networks. Additionally, think about hosting fundraising events in your local community.

Work-Study Or Internships: If considering an international internship, ask if the position is paid. Some internships offer a stipend, which can help offset costs. Alternatively, if studying abroad, ask your program about work-study opportunities or part-time jobs available to students.

Budgeting & Saving: Never underestimate the power of good budgeting and saving habits! Plan your expenses, cut unnecessary costs, and save a portion of any money earned from part-time jobs. Over time, this money can accumulate and become a considerable part of your travel fund.

Remember, while the cost of travel and studying abroad might seem disheartening, do not let it discourage you. With some research, planning, and creativity, there are numerous ways to fund these invaluable experiences. Your investment in these experiences will pay dividends through the skills, perspectives, and connections gained.

Plan Ahead: Think About Your Resume!

You may feel it is too early to start compiling your resume in the first year of college. However, it is never too early to begin because building skills and experiences take time. One major reason to gain soft skills, pursue work experience, and participate in extracurricular activities during college is that these experiences can be used to create a solid and impressive resume. This resume becomes your primary tool for showcasing your value to potential employers, helping you stand out in a competitive job market.

Work Experience: A solid resume is about more than just grades or degrees. It reflects your experiences, skills, and accomplishments. Every internship, part-time job, or co-op role can speak volumes about you. The work done can be used as examples to show potential employers how you have tackled challenges, collaborated with others, or demonstrated leadership skills. These provide practical evidence of your ability and readiness to perform well in a professional environment.

Soft Skills: The transferable skills gained have increasingly become decisive factors for employers. These abilities are not industry-specific but are applicable across the board, making you a versatile candidate capable of thriving in diverse work environments.

Extracurricular Activities: Involvement in non-academic activities adds a unique flavor to your resume and can make you stand out from the crowd. Participation in clubs, sports, or community service not only suggests a well-rounded individual, but also demonstrates commitment, teamwork, leadership, and the ability to juggle multiple responsibilities.

Traveling, Studying Abroad & Overseas Volunteering: These experiences signify adaptability, a global perspective, and a broader understanding of diversity, which are highly desirable qualities in today's interconnected world.

Combined, these experiences and skills shape your brand and the story you present to potential employers. It is not just about checking off boxes on a list of qualifications but demonstrating how your unique journey has equipped you for the position you are applying for. The aim is to paint a picture of a dynamic, competent, and well-rounded candidate who has the potential to bring much to the table. Every step taken and every experience gained during your college years contributes to building a solid resume that showcases the experiences and qualities that future employers are looking for.

Peers & Alumni: The Power Of Networking

The benefit of networking cannot be underestimated. This concept was first mentioned during Chapter 3: Orientation Week because of the advantages of starting at the earliest opportunity. Networking is an integral part of preparing for post-college life, and it should not be viewed as a chore but instead as a fun social activity. It involves establishing connections with professionals in your field and with the people you meet in daily student life. Two key networking groups should be considered: your peers and the alumni from your institution.

Peers: These are fellow students with whom you study, engage in projects or extracurricular activities, and form friendships. Your classmates might become industry leaders, entrepreneurs, or professionals across various fields. Building solid relationships with them now can lead to future collaborations, opportunities, and support networks. In a way, peers can become allies in your career journey, providing mutual assistance and sharing valuable information and opportunities.

Alumni: These connections are like a bridge between your current college experience and the professional world. These individuals have walked your path, experiencing the challenges and successes of transitioning from student life to a professional career. They can provide insights, advice, and perhaps job opportunities that might not be found elsewhere. Alumni often have a sense of loyalty to their alma mater, so they are usually willing to help students from the same institution.

In both cases, networking is more than just asking for a job. It is about learning, better understanding your chosen field, and forming connections. Remember networking is a two-way street; it is as much about how you can help others as how they can help you.

So, start cultivating these relationships as soon as you can. Attend networking events, join clubs and societies, become an active college community member, and don't hesitate to reach out to alumni. Building a robust network can open up opportunities and give you a significant advantage when ready to enter the job market.

Networking Opportunities

Networking in college is not just about collecting business cards or finding job opportunities but about making genuine connections. Start early because it gives you more time to meet diverse, interesting people with their own stories and insights. A recap of the best ways to network include:

Clubs & Societies: Being an active member of student clubs and societies connects you with like-minded individuals. These organizations often also provide opportunities to interact with professionals in the field who are invited to give guest lectures or seminars.

Campus Events: Universities often host networking events, workshops, and career fairs. These are fantastic opportunities to meet industry professionals, alumni, and fellow students. Don't hesitate to introduce yourself and engage in conversations.

Alumni: Take advantage of your college's alumni networks. Attend alumni-student events, reach out for informational interviews, or seek a mentor among alumni already established in your career field.

Social Media: Do not underestimate the benefits of online networking platforms like LinkedIn, X, and Facebook. Connect with people in your field, follow industry leaders, share thoughts on relevant topics, and reach out to those whose career paths interest you. Regularly share and participate with content related to your field of interest.

Work Experience: Internships, volunteering, part-time jobs, and work-study opportunities are also great for networking. They help you meet and work with professionals and gain practical insights into the industry.

Classroom Connections: Do not forget to network in your classes. Build relationships with classmates and professors. You never know how these connections may help in the future.

Social Events: Believe it or not, social activities like parties, campus festivals, or sports practices can provide excellent occasions to network! In these relaxed settings, engaging with peers and seniors on a personal level can be easier. This can enable stronger, more genuine connections that could become professional in the future. Be open and interested in others, and do not be shy about sharing your interests and ambitions.

How To Be A Super Networker

Becoming an ace networker in college can be an empowering and worthwhile experience with the right approach and mindset. Networking should not be viewed as a big deal or a serious event. Think of it as a casual coffee chat or a relaxed hangout. After all, it is just about getting to know people and letting them get to know you. Embrace it as a fun, social part of your college journey. Here is a reminder of some ways to network successfully:

Start Early: Begin networking at the start of college. Orientation Week is an excellent opportunity to meet new people looking to make connections. Attend events, join clubs, and participate in discussions that will put you in contact with a diverse range of people.

Be Prepared: Do homework before attending networking events - know who will be there and what you want to achieve. Having a few questions or conversation starters ready beforehand can help break the ice.

Quality Over Quantity: Focus on meaningful connections not the number of events. Aim for deeper conversations with fewer people.

Reciprocity: Networking is a two-way street. Always consider what you can offer others, whether time, skills, or knowledge.

Be Genuine: Authenticity goes a long way when building relationships. Show genuine interest in others by listening to what they say and responding thoughtfully.

Master The Art of Small Talk: While it may seem trivial, small talk can lead to deeper conversations. Being comfortable with small talk can help you navigate social situations more smoothly.

Practice Active Listening: Being able to listen to others is crucial. It shows respect, builds trust, and helps you understand the other person's perspective.

Follow-Up: After meeting someone, sending a brief note or email to express appreciation for the conversation or event is always a good idea. This can help establish a long-term relationship.

Maintain Your Network: Networking is not a one-time event - keeping in touch with the connections made is recommended. Send articles they may find interesting, congratulate them on achievements or milestones, and do not be afraid to seek advice or guidance.

Networking is about building relationships, gaining insights from others' experiences, and finding common ground. Be authentic, show interest, and follow up after initial meetings or conversations. Remember that reciprocity is essential, so think about how you can also help others. Networking often happens naturally when it is part of something enjoyable. So, get out there, get involved, and start making those connections. You never know where they might lead in the future!

Embrace Lifelong Learning

Learning never stops; it is a vital aspect of personal and professional growth that extends beyond university years. It is about recognizing that education does not finish at graduation. Instead, it is an ongoing process that continues throughout life. Here is why embracing this mindset is so important:

Adaptability: Change is the only constant in today's fast-paced world. Technologies evolve, industries transform, and job roles get redefined. You must keep up with these changes to remain current and competitive in your career. Lifelong learning allows you to adapt, whether mastering a new software tool, understanding emerging trends in your industry, or even transitioning to a different career.

Enhances Career Prospects: Continuously updating your skillset and acquiring new competencies can increase your value to your current company and improve your appeal to other employers. Whether earning professional qualifications, attending workshops, or taking online courses, every bit of learning can boost your career.

Personal Development: Lifelong learning is also about personal growth. Knowledge and continued education can broaden perspectives and enrich your life and understanding of the world. Examples could be learning a new language, playing a musical instrument, or understanding how to invest in the stock market.

Boosts Confidence: The more you learn, the more competent and confident you become. This positivity can spill over into all aspects of your life, improving work performance, relationships, and problem-solving skills.

Stay Engaged & Curious: Lifelong learning keeps you mentally engaged and satisfies your natural curiosity. This can lead to fulfillment and happiness, thereby positively impacting mental health.

To embrace lifelong learning, start by cultivating curiosity about the world around you. Seek learning opportunities through formal education, books, seminars, podcasts, or conversations with individuals from diverse backgrounds. Most importantly, keep an open mind, as you never know where your learning journey may take you.

College isn't just about academics; it is a place to plan and shape your future. Embrace a growth mindset and set specific goals to turn your experiences there into stepping stones for your career. Delve into extracurriculars and work experiences to develop crucial soft skills and create a robust professional network of peers and alumni.

Undecided about a career? Use college as a testing ground to find your passion. If further studies align with your goals, plan accordingly, considering the investment commitment. Also, travel or study abroad where possible to gain a global outlook.

Remember, learning doesn't stop at graduation. Lifelong learning keeps you adaptable and sharp, ready for the evolving job market. So, keep learning, stay curious, and build a foundation now for lifelong success!

Chapter 13

The End Is Just The Beginning

" The best way to predict your future is to create it."

Abraham Lincoln

Now we have reached the end of this guide, it is time to take a step back and review the overall college experience. It is a rich, vibrant tapestry woven with threads of academics, personal development, social connections, and preparation for your future. Each thread is essential; how you weave them together will define your unique college journey.

Remember that college is more than just a pathway to a degree. It is a place for growth, an opportunity to explore, and a time to challenge yourself. It is about honing academic abilities to succeed in your chosen field and developing the transferable skills to make you stand out in today's competitive job market.

Be brave and have the courage to step out of your comfort zone! Explore new opportunities by engaging in extracurricular activities and internships, networking with peers and alumni, and studying abroad. These experiences are crucial for developing valuable life skills, shaping your identity, and enhancing your resume.

Remember that planning can be your best friend when it comes to succeeding in your academic goals. Setting clear objectives and aligning your educational progress with these goals is essential. Monitoring your progress to ensure you remain on track is also crucial. At the same time, learn to be flexible. College is also about discovering your true passion, so be open to new ideas, interests, and career paths.

Making friends is a unique and invaluable aspect of your college years. The shared late-night study sessions, campus adventures, and fun moments create strong bonds and shared memories. So, be sure to value and nurture these connections; they are not only for the present but can endure a lifetime.

Mastering your finances and budgeting is as crucial as your academic pursuits. It is not just about saving pennies; the good habits formed during college can set you on a path to financial security.

Cultivate lifelong learning. Remember, graduation is not the end of your educational journey but just the beginning. The world is rapidly changing, and to keep up, you must learn and adapt continuously. Pursue professional qualifications, attend workshops, and above all, stay curious.

Finally, remember to enjoy this special period in your life. College is a time for learning, personal growth, and fun - make the most of it! Prioritize your physical and mental well-being, establish meaningful connections with others, and cherish the memories you make along the way.

With these strategies and guidelines, you are now well-equipped to navigate your journey through college and beyond. Embrace the challenges, learn from the failures, celebrate the victories, and most importantly, always keep learning. Here's to a successful and fulfilling college life, and a future filled with endless possibilities.

Finally, I hope you achieve great success, happiness, and prosperity in all your future endeavors. Best wishes to you!

Notepad

Download Your Free Checklists & Budget Spreadsheet

Grab your Free Printable Checklists, Moving Timetable, and Customizable Budgeting Spreadsheet Here!

Scan the QR code to access your downloads and subscribe to our updates.

Or visit https://bit.ly/uni-college-guide

REFERENCES

Jubbal, K. (2022). *7 Evidence-Based Study Strategies (And How to Use Each).* Med School Insiders. https://medschoolinsiders.com/study-strategies/7-evidence-based-study-strategies-how-to-use-each/

Nero, C.A. & Zulkiply, N. (2021). *The Effects of Retrieval Practice Across Levels of Thinking and Retention Interval on Reading Comprehension.* AJUE. https://files.eric.ed.gov/fulltext/EJ1327865.pdf

Walck-Shannon, E., Rowell, S. F., & Frey, R. F. (2021). *To What Extent Do Study Habits Relate To Performance?* CBE Life Sciences Education, 20(1), ar6. https://doi.org/10.1187/cbe.20-05-0091

Dunlosky, J. , Rawson, K.A, & Willingham, D.T (2013). *Improving Students' Learning With Effective Learning Techniques: Promising Directions From Cognitive and Educational Psychology.* Sage Journals. https://journals.sagepub.com/doi/10.1177/1529100612453266

Doran, G. T. (1981). *There's a S.M.A.R.T. Way to Write Management's Goals and Objectives.* Management Review. 70 (11): 35–36. https://scirp.org/reference/referencespapers?referenceid=2982408

Eisenhower. (2017, February 7). *The Eisenhower Matrix: Introduction & 3-Minute Video Tutorial.* Eisenhower -. https://www.eisenhower.me/eisenhower-matrix/

Cirillo, F (2018). *The Pomodoro Technique: The Acclaimed Time-Management System That| Has Transformed How We Work.* Penguin Random House. http://pomodorotechnique.com/book-pomodoro-technique.php

Pace, K.L., MSU Extension. (2017, March 31). *The Myth of Multitasking: Research Says it Makes Us Less Productive and Increases Mistakes.* https://www.canr.msu.edu/news/the_myth_of _multitasking_research _says_it_makes_us_less_productive_and_increases mistakes

USC (2023) *Are There Benefits of Multitasking?* /USC MAPP Online https://appliedpsychologydegree.usc.edu /blog/benefits-of-multitasking

Cleveland Clinic (2024, April 1). *Why Multitasking Doesn't Work.* https://health.clevelandclinic.org /science-clear-multitasking-doesnt-work/

Cornell Health. (n.d.). *Study Breaks & Stress-Busters* https://health.cornell.edu/about/news/study-breaks-stress-busters

Buzan, T., & Buzan, B. (1993). *The Mind Map Book: How to Use Radiant Thinking to Maximize Your Brain's Untapped Potential.* Plume.

OnlineSchools.org. (n.d.). *The Science of Taking a Break.* https://www.onlineschools.org/science-of-study-breaks/

Carr, L. L., PhD. (2023, July 21). *Study Smart by Taking Breaks that Refresh* - https://www.linkedin.com/pulse/study-smart-taking-breaks-refresh-linda-larson-carr-ph-d-

UNC-Chapel Hill Learning Center. (2024, February 19). *Taking Breaks.* Learning Center. https://learningcenter.unc.edu/tips-and-tools/taking-breaks/

Maryville University (2022). *8 Study Break Ideas That Can Help Boost Your Learning* (https://online.maryville.edu/blog/study-break-ideas/

Indeed (2023). *How To Take a Break From Studying (And Why It's Important).* https://www.indeed.com/career-advice/career-development/how-to-take-break-from-studying

Neuroscience News. (2021, July 29). *Remember More by Taking Breaks.* https://neurosciencenews.com/long-break-memory-19015/

Teachers1on1 (2021, November 8) *How taking Frequent Breaks can Improve Memory.* https://www.teachers1on1.com/blog/taking-frequent-breaks-improve-memory

Scott, E., PhD. (2023, November 9). *How to Take a Break from Work (and Why You Need To).* Verywell Mind. https://www.verywellmind.com/why-you-should-take-a-break-3144576

National Institutes of Health (NIH) (2021, June 29). *How Short Breaks Help The Brain Learn New Skills.* https://www.nih.gov/news-events/nih-research-matters/how-short-breaks-help-brain-learn-new-skills

UCL (2020, September 17). *5 Benefits of Taking Breaks.* https://www.ucl.ac.uk/students/news/2020/feb/5-benefits-taking-breaks

Chick, N. (2013). *Metacognition.* Vanderbilt University Center for Teaching. Retrieved April 2024 from https://cft.vanderbilt.edu/guides-sub-pages/metacognition/.

LINCS (n.d.). *TEAL Center Fact Sheet No. 4: Metacognitive processes.* Adult Education and Literacy | U.S. Department of Education. https://lincs.ed.gov/state-resources/federal-initiatives/teal/guide/metacognitive

Medina, M. S., Castleberry, A. N., & Persky, A. M. (2017). *Strategies for Improving Learner Metacognition in Health Professional Education.* American Journal of Pharmaceutical Education, 81(4), 78. https://doi.org/10.5688/ajpe81478

How People Learn. (2000). In National Academies Press eBooks. https://doi.org/10.17226/9853

Getting started with Metacognition. **(n.d.).** https://cambridge-community.org.uk/professional-development/gswmeta/index.html

Brame, C. (2013). *Thinking About Metacognition.* Vanderbilt University. https://cft.vanderbilt.edu/2013/01/thinking-about-metacognition/

Samani, J., & Pan, S. C. (2021). *Interleaved Practice Enhances Memory and Problem-Solving Ability in Undergraduate Physics.* NPJ Science of Learning, 6(1). https://doi.org/10.1038/s41539-021-00110-x

Young, A. (2023, March 15). *Interleaving: Boost learning by mixing your studying.* Alexander Young. https://blog.alexanderfyoung.com/interleaving/

Wadsworth, W. (2021, May 28). *Interleaved Practice 101: What Really is Interleaving and How to REALLY Use It In Teaching and Learning.* Exam Study Expert. https://examstudyexpert.com/interleaving/

Shatz, I. (n.d.). *Interleaving: How Mixed Practice Can Boost Learning.* Effectiviology. https://effectiviology.com/interleaving/

Wazir, A., Sya'ban, S.N. & Horneffer, P. (2021). *Interleaving: How to Mix Related Concepts to Make Learning in Medicine More Durable.* Lecturio. https://www.lecturio.com/pulse/interleaving-how-to-mix-related-concepts-to-make-learning-in-medicine-more-durable/

5 Easy Ways to Use Dual Coding for Studying. Inner Drive. Retrieved 14 Dec 2023 from https://blog.innerdrive.co.uk/5-ways-to-use-dual-coding

Sumeracki, M. (2023, September 18). *Dual Coding and Learning Styles.* The Learning Scientists. https://www.learningscientists.org/blog/2019/6/6-1

Smith, M. & Weinstein, Y. (2016). *Learn How To Study Using Dual Coding.* Learning Scientists. https://www.learningscientists.org/blog/2016/9/1-1

Structural Learning. (2021, October 26). *Dual Coding: A Teacher's Guide.* https://www.structural-learning.com/post/dual-coding-a-teachers-guide

Clark, M. (2021). *What is Dual Coding Theory and How Can It Help Teaching?.* Century. https://www.century.tech/news/what-is-dual-coding-theory-and-how-can-it-help-teaching/

Explaining the Dual Coding Theory (2018). Simple Show. Retrieved 14 Dec 2023 from https://simpleshow.com/blog/explain-dual-coding-theory/

Spacing Effect (n.d.). The Decision Lab. Retrieved 14 Dec 2023 from https://thedecisionlab.com/biases/spacing-effect

Winerman, L. (2011). *Study Smart.* APA. https://www.apa.org/gradpsych/2011/11/study-smart

Salovey, P., & Mayer, J. D. (1990). *Emotional Intelligence.* Basic Books.

Printed in Great Britain
by Amazon

52766276R00126